HOW TO STUDY AND LIKE IT
Orientation to Learning

by

Mabry G. Blaylock
Counselor and Professional Tutor
B.A. in Letters, M.A., Member of Phi Beta Kappa
University of Oklahoma, Norman, Oklahoma

Los Angeles  California

ABOUT THE AUTHOR

Mabry Blaylock was born on a farm near Hammon, in western Oklahoma, where he spent his youth. He now lives with his mother in Norman, where he tutors students of the University of Oklahoma and, occasionally, students of Norman High School. When anyone mentions the Phi Beta Kappa key he won in his junior year, he laughs it off, saying, "That's the result of the seven years I spent getting a good high-school background."

The real story is a little more involved. When he was fourteen, Mabry sustained a paralyzing injury in a hunting accident during Christmas vacation of his sophomore year in high school. As he convalesced, he read extensively and studied Spanish "for kicks," but he didn't accept the fact that he wasn't going to be walking back to Hammon High School someday. It wasn't until some three years after his injury that he got busy with his last two and a half years of high-school work by correspondence study through the University of Oklahoma.

After graduation from high school, he spent almost a year in a hospital and entered the University in a wheelchair a few months after he was old enough to vote. At the University, Mabry kept up the almost perfect grade average he had made as a correspondence student, taking a Bachelor of Arts in Letters and a Master of Arts in Spanish within five years. He worked a year as an assistant copy editor at the University of Oklahoma Press before he turned to tutoring math, through calculus, and a wide range of other freshman and sophomore courses.

Mabry Blaylock has now tutored professionally for more than ten years, sharing the secrets of method and attitude that he has discovered as a student, as a teacher of himself, and as a tutor and counselor for more than two thousand students, a few of whom have won their own Phi Beta Kappa keys.

DEDICATED TO

Mother and Dad,
who got me started,
and
Walter Campbell and Foster-Harris,
who helped point the way.

ACKNOWLEDGEMENTS

No one lives his life alone. In thinking of persons who have contributed significantly to my life and indirectly to my writing this book, dozens and dozens of names come quickly to mind — names of relatives, neighbors, schoolmates, teachers, professors, physicians, nurses, students, friends. To include all their names would fill pages with names unfamiliar to all but a few of the readers of this book.

I limit this acknowledgement, therefore, to two names of persons directly involved in my writing and publishing *How to Study and Like It*. First, I credit much of its clarity and readability to Professor Foster-Harris, who read the entire manuscript, asking clarifying questions and making constructive criticism. Second, I thank Joseph Lawrence, Editor, Crescent Publications, Inc., for his unfailing consideration and promptness in our correspondence leading to publication of this book.

Finally, I express my deep appreciation to George Obligado for permission to use excerpts from his article "The Most Unforgettable Character I've Met." Excerpts used with permission from the February 1963 *Reader's Digest*. Copyright 1963 by the Reader's Digest Assn., Inc.

M.B.

INTRODUCTION: FINDING YOUR WAY AROUND

Do you remember how you felt that very first day in college? Or if you are about to start for the first time, you probably feel the same way. Lost!

Nearly all students seem to feel about the same on that first day. You are not at all unusual if you get butterflies in your stomach when you look up and down the tree-lined streets, gaze at the somewhat forbidding-looking buildings, and fully realize for the first time that you are a student here.

Remembering stories of embarrassed freshmen who can't locate their first classes, you wonder unhappily whether you will be able to find your way around by the end of the first day. You notice the other students around you, and you think you can tell the upperclassmen from the freshmen. The freshmen look as puzzled and as uncertain as you feel. The upperclassmen appear to know where they are going and what they are doing. You feel a twinge of envy. You watch pipe-smoking professors head for the library, a building that's a little frightening because of all the knowledge and learning it represents. You wonder if there is ever an end to all this learning.

When you get your pack of registration materials, you sigh with relief on seeing a map of the campus. At least you will know which building is which. Maybe it won't take long to find your way from classroom to classroom, from dormitory to library.

You wish it were as easy to find ways to use the learning represented by your college, by its books and periodicals, by its administration and faculty members. You think of stories you have heard about student difficulties and successes. You long for something to point the way for you, a kind of map or compass that will give you a sense of direction in facing the problems before you — studying, writing themes and reports, learning languages, solving mathematical problems, taking notes in class, taking exams, and organizing your time.

Well, freshman or not, you've found this book. You hope it will provide some of the direction that you seek, and I hope with you! Perhaps, though, you're expecting it to reveal something impossible—a shortcut to knowledge, a royal road to learning. *There isn't any.*

I do not pretend that the ideas and suggestions in this book can substitute for hard, interested effort on your part. Instead, these pages will provide you with suggestions that I—and hundreds of my students—have found useful. After you have studied, absorbed, and put these suggestions to use, you may discover that they *have* provided you with the sense of direction that you are now hoping to find for your college or high-school work or for your self-directed study.

The sections of this book will not all be of equal value to you. You may already be a whiz at math, and you may read rapidly through the math section for a few ideas. Or math may be difficult for you, and you may want to study that section several times. You are almost certain, I think, to find useful the section on theme and essay writing.

In short, you'll find that some parts of this book "are to be tasted, others to be swallowed, and some few to be chewed and digested." Through a quick reading you will find which parts are which for you.

So, read on, and may you find the guidance you are seeking.

CONTENTS

HOW TO STUDY AND LIKE IT
Orientation to Learning

CHAPTER 1

START WHERE YOU ARE:
The Personal-Experience Theme

"I've got to write a theme, and I don't know where to start."
You're bound to hear someone say this, and when you do,
you'll have heard the most common complaint of college
freshmen.

All a person can write about is what he knows. You're up
against the kind of problem St. Francis of Assisi was talking
about way back in the thirteenth century when he said, "The
only knowledge a man has is what he can put to use." And the
average person knows enough and has experienced enough to
fill a shelf full of novels, to say nothing of
three-to-five-hundred-word themes.

So the answer to the question about where to start is this:
"Start where you are."

I reached this useful conclusion many years ago, when I was
enrolled in freshman English through correspondence study and
faced the same kind of problem. I had just finished the second
lesson and didn't know what kind of punishment to expect

3

from the third. At least that's the way I felt about it. You couldn't tell what a spinster Ph.D. in English might dream up.

Bravely, I flipped to the assignment. "Read 'Summer Moods,' by George Gissing," it said. Sounds nice and sweet like something an old-maid schoolteacher would want to read, I thought. "Write a theme of between 500 and 1000 words, imitating Part I of 'Summer Moods.' Be more sensuous than Gissing if possible."

"Isn't it enough to assign a theme of five hundred to a thousand words without using words I'll have to look up?" I wondered. Looking at the word *sensuous* again, I grew a little more interested. "Hmmm, doesn't *sensuous* have something to do with sex?" I asked myself. Maybe "Summer Moods" wouldn't be so bad after all.

But Webster showed that it didn't necessarily have anything to do with sex. According to my dictionary, *sensuous* meant "characterized by sense perception or imagery addressed to the senses." I took the word to mean "rich in words referring to things you could see, hear, touch, taste, and smell."

A little disappointed, I closed the dictionary, turned to "Summer Moods," and started to read.

To-day, as I was reading in the garden, a waft of summer perfume *[how tender, I thought]*—some hidden kind of association in what I read—I know not what it may have been—took me back to schoolboy holidays; I recovered with strange intensity that lightsome mood of long release from tasks, of going away to the seaside, which is one of childhood's blessings.

Finally a period, but not the end of the paragraph. "What is he doing?" I asked myself. "Sounds like—what's the word?—*nostalgia.* That's it, nostalgia." I read on.

I was in the train; no rushing express such as bears you great distances; the sober train which goes to no place of importance, which lets you see the white steam of the engine float and fall upon a meadow ere you pass. *[At last, here's something you can really see.]* . . .At every station

4

the train stopped; little stations decked with flowers
[something else you can see], smelling warm in the
sunshine *[ah, something you can smell]*, where
countryfolk got in with baskets, talked in an unfamiliar
dialect *[something you can hear]*, an English which to us
sounded almost like a foreign tongue. Then the first
glimpse of the sea *[sight again]*; the excitement of noting
whether the tide was high or low—stretches of sand and
weedy pools *[nice and specific]*, or halcyon *[don't forget
to look this one up]* wavelets frothing at their furthest
reach, under the sea-banks starred with convolvulus *[with
what?]*. Of a sudden, *our* station!

Ah, that taste of brine on a child's lips! *[Taste, of
course.]* Nowadays, I can take a holiday when I will and to
whithersoever it pleases me; but that salt kiss *[taste and
touch]* of the sea air I shall never know again. . . . Were it
possible, but for one half-hour, to plunge and bask in the
sunny surf *[touch]*, to roll on the silvery sand hills *[touch
and sight]*, to leap from rock to rock on shining sea-ferns,
laughing if I slipped into the shallows among starfish and
anemones! . . .*

"Well, there wasn't so much there that you could see, hear,
touch, taste, or smell," I thought. It might not be so hard to be
"more sensuous than Gissing" after all.

But I certainly couldn't imitate the seashore bit. I had never
seen the seashore in my life. The nostalgia, the recollection of
childhood, the way he got into his subject—these I might be
able to imitate. I decided to close up shop on English for the
day and sleep on the problem.

I was almost asleep that night when I found myself thinking
about the theme assignment again. A waft of perfume had set
Gissing off. I wondered what I could use to get myself started.

The Private Papers of Henry Ryecroft, by George Gissing, published by E. P.
Dutton & Co., Inc., New York, 1903. Reprinted in *Practice in Reading and Writing,*
by Clark Emery, John L. Lievsay, and Henry F. Thoma, Houghton Mifflin Company,
New York, 1942, p. 8.

Looking sleepily around me, I noticed that my room was almost filled with moonlight. That was an idea. I could hear frogs croaking. That was specific enough for a sound image. The night was warm, but now and then a breeze cooled the room. That was touch. I had my start; I'd see what I could do with it the next day.

The ideas that seem brilliant at night sometimes fade in the daylight. When I got ready to write it down, the moonlight idea didn't seem very good.

I stared at the wall for about five minutes, occasionally rubbing the back of my head—but nothing. "You've got to get started," I told myself. "Write something!" So, remembering my idea of the night before, I wrote:

Last night after I had lain awake for several minutes thinking about and making plans for the future *[this would get me started and set the stage, so to speak]*, I became aware of moonlight streaming into my room.

That didn't look too bad for a starter, I thought. But where could I go from here? "Be more sensuous than Gissing," I remembered. Okay, I'd throw in some sensuous images. Continuing the same paragraph, I wrote, "The peaceful stillness *[no sound]* of a warm night *[touch]* was broken only by some frogs' hoarse croaking."

That didn't sound as flowery as Gissing, I thought. How could I pretty it up for a nice English teacher? Oh, I had it. Frogs usually croaked for a rain, but it was drier than a Fourth-of-July firecracker. So what could the stupid animals be croaking for? "For a rain." That was sentence fragment, though. I couldn't get away with that. So I erased a period and a capital F, and now the sentence was "The peaceful stillness of a warm night was broken only by some frogs' hoarse croaking for a rain."

I read the sentence aloud. It still didn't sound quite right to me. I tried "for a rain to wet the soil." I needed some two-dollar expressions to please a nice old English teacher. After some more thought, I finally felt I had what I wanted:

The peaceful stillness of a warm night was broken only by some frogs' hoarse croaking for a rain to quench the thirst of the parched land.

I read it over aloud. "Now, that was pretty good," I thought. I doubted if Gissing could have done better.

I had written some fairly long sentences. I guessed it would be good to have a short one. What else had I been able to hear the night before? Nothing. So I wrote, "All else was silence."

Any other sensations? Well, there had been a cool breeze now and then. So expressing it as an English teacher might like it, I ventured, "The breath of the slightest breeze cooled my cheek."

"So far, it's pretty good," I thought. But then I frowned and scratched my head trying to think of where to go from there. "Warm moonlit night . . . warm moonlit night. How about a little contrast?" I asked myself. Answering my own question, I came up with "cold, dark mornings."

What about cold, moonlit mornings? I hated to get up, for one thing. I could just hear that old dollar alarm clock buzzing in my ear before real daylight. Why so early? Because my brother and I had to get up and do what we called "juicing the cows" and the other chores in time to get ready to walk a mile to school. A description of waking up and crawling out of bed ought to be good for one paragraph, I decided. But I needed a sentence or two to connect the ideas.

I thought I'd latch the transition onto the first paragraph so my theme wouldn't come back marked for lack of paragraph development. Throwing in a mathematical comparison, I finally came up with a couple of sentences that might rate as a fair imitation of Gissing.

Thoughts about the future became lost in a flood of memories of my younger days. By some strange formula of memorial arithmetic, moonlight plus a warm stillness equalled memories not of a similar summer night but of the frosty *[touch]*, moonlit *[sight]* mornings when my brother and I used to get up before dawn to do the chores. The next paragraph pretty well wrote itself. First, I added a

7

sentence to link this paragraph to the last sentence of the one before: "I was soon transported back to such a morning."

Then, using moonlight and the ringing of an alarm clock as a starting point, I continued:

The moonlight was streaming into my room as I awakened to the insistent ringing *[sound]* of a dollar alarm clock.

What next? Why not include my reaction, so I put down:

I might have turned over in the cozy comfort *[touch]* of bed, and would have gone back to sleep, but my brother soon became more insistent than the clock that I get up.

At this point I was much tempted to write about stepping onto the icy-cold floor and slipping into heavy, long-handled underwear. But remembering the Gissing example, and thinking my teacher might not like anything quite so blunt, I decided to skip the mundane process of dressing. As I wrote on, I tried to switch attention from what was outside me to my reactions within.

To leave a warm *[touch]* bed on a frosty *[constrast]* morning was to test my will power to the utmost. But how invigorated *[contrast again]* I felt as the heavy clothing became warm around my body and I followed my brother into the crisp outdoor freshness of the early morning air!

Now that I'd gotten myself outside the house, how was I going to work in a little movement and more of those sensuous details? After I stared at the wall a while longer, I shut my eyes for a moment, and then a whole flock of images concerned with moonlight and early-morning chores came to mind—twinkling stars, light in the east, roosters crowing, coyotes howling, owls hooting. The next paragraph came easily.

As we crunched *[action, sound]* through the snow, I could see the snow-covered hills to the west merging almost imperceptibly *[a big, English-teacher type of word, I thought]* into the sky. In the east a rosy dawn *[sight]* heralded the approach of a new day. Overhead twinkling stars *[sight]* were beginning to fade; the nearly full moon *[sight]* was fast apporaching the horizon. In the cow lot, the milch cows lowed *[sound]* for their feed and to be milked. Roosters in the poultry houses crowed *[sound]* their good-mornings. An owl perched high in a bare cottonwood tree hooted sleepily *[sight and sound]*. A coyote in a pasture nearby howled *[sound]* as if in protest to man's encroachment upon his domain *[I used a dictionary and a thesaurus to come up with these fancy words]*.

I looked at the paragraph as written so far. It seemed to me that an English teacher would want a sentence that would summarize what was going on. Owls, coyotes were—let's see—nocturnal animals. What was the word opposite to nocturnal? I couldn't think of one. So back to the dictionary for synonyms and antonyms. *Diurnal* looked pretty good. I'd better make sure of its meaning, though, because an English teacher thinks nothing shows your ignorance more than a big word used incorrectly. I looked up *diurnal:* "related to the daytime, opposed to nocturnal." Just what I wanted. I then wrote the concluding sentence.

"Nocturnal animals were ceasing their activities; diurnal animals were beginning theirs."

It was simple, but it had a couple of two-dollar words that the teacher might like. What next? I could have written about the barnyard odors, but Gissing hadn't had any unpleasant images, and teacher might not like them either. So I decided to leave out the odors and a bit about stepping carefully through the cow lot to keep my shoes clean.

What happened after the chores were done? Breakfast. Good, that would give me a chance to bring in taste and smell images. I would just summarize the part about doing the chores and then get my brother and me back to breakfast:

Soon we had all thirteen *[quite specific]* of the cows milked and fed, and the chickens fed and watered.

"Soon" gave me a transition in time, and "cows" and "chickens" tied in with the preceding paragraph. I continued:

9

How to Study and Like It

My brother and I returned to the house with large pails laden with foamy white milk *[sight]*, with cold feet *[touch]*, and with a ravishing appetite, an appetite that can be produced only by activity in the freshness of early morning *[even a schoolteacher would have had this kind of experience]*. It wasn't long *[you can't get away with a contraction with some teachers, but I'd give it a try]* before we were consuming the hot biscuits *[sight, touch, taste, smell]*, the tender ham and eggs *[same]*, the hot chocolate, and the steaming oatmeal *[my mouth watered just writing about it]* that Mother had prepared for us as we did the chores.

I needed a sentence to wrap up the paragraph. First I tried, "Food never tasted better to people who make a practice of eating good food." Then, after using a dictionary and a thesaurus, I came up with a sentence I liked much better: "Food never tasted more delicious to the most fastidious gourmet."

I needed another paragraph or two to make my theme long enough, but I was stuck again. I didn't want to get too far from moonlight or summer. Then I thought of trying another twist, from moonlit winter mornings to sunny summer afternoons. I couldn't think of anything more fun than a summer swim. But again I'd have to work up a transition.

I remembered a little device with a big name—a kaleidoscope—that somebody had given me once. It occurred to me that flashing from one set of images to another was a little like holding a kaleidoscope up to the light and turning it to get an endless number of colorful geometric figures. "Memory is like a kaleidoscope," I wrote. Then I decided to shorten that phrase to "kaleidoscope of memory." I was pleased with that. With a transition phrase in mind, I visualized myself going off for a swim, and I wrote my next paragraph.

In the kaleidoscope of memory, space and time are conquered. Soon the scene had shifted, winter had changed into summer, and I was trudging over miles of

10

rough pasture with my brother and two cousins *[nice, specific number]* to go swimming in a pond. In my memory the cracked mud at the edge of the pond *[sight]* again tickled my feet *[if you've ever walked on such mud, you'll never forget the feeling].* Cool water *[touch]* splashed over our shoulders as we churned *[movement, sight, sound]* through the water to see who could reach the opposite bank first.

Then what? I couldn't stop just here, but I felt I had written about enough to prove I could be "more sensuous than Gissing." I started my theme with thinking about the future. How about having my brother and cousins and me talking about the future way back then? So I continued:

> Water got in our eyes and hair, but we didn't mind. After we became tired old Sol smiled down on our backs as we lay in the green grass *[sight]* talking and dreaming of things we planned to do "when we got grown."

I thought about ending the theme here, but it didn't feel quite right. What was wrong? This last paragraph tied in only with the first sentence of the first paragraph. I was still remembering things. How about coming full circle—as you go out and return home—back to the moonlight and the frogs? That seemed like a pretty good idea.

I thought about a transition. Getting shaken out of a daydream was sometimes pretty startling, and getting shaken awake from a real dream was worse. Maybe I could get a little of the same kind of effect by not using a transition at all. I did want to show, though, that a good deal of time had passed while I was remembering all these things. So I began my last paragraph.

> In my room the flood of moonlight had become a small shaft of light. The breeze had all but stopped stirring. Outside the frogs still croaked as I wondered sleepily what time it was.

So far, so good, I felt. How about for a fade out, a real fancy sentence to please a woman English teacher? I jotted down two or three sentences and chose one of them to conclude:

Memory poured over memory until I slipped into that enchanted state of the past and future called dreamland.

It sounded real schoolgirlish, I thought, but I believed teacher would like it, and she was the only one I had to please.

The next thing to do was to find a title, and then I'd be through except for a final check of what I'd written and, of course, the final draft. I scribbled a number of possible titles—"Back When I Was Younger," "Summer Thoughts," "Summer and Winter," and "Memories on a Summer Night." But I didn't like any of these very well. Scratching my head for an idea didn't seem to help. So I went back, finally, to Roget's *Thesaurus.* Under *memory* I found the word that I thought fitted best, and I titled my theme "Reminiscences."

Now I had my title. Before writing the final draft, I'd check my work against a set of instructions I'd made for myself and had pasted in front of my English book.

13 Rules for Writing Themes

1) Read the assignment carefully.
2) Follow the assignment.
3) On the first draft, leave spaces between lines for changes and corrections.
4) Write on something you already know a good deal about, if possible.
5) Keep thinking of the reader's probable reactions.
6) Keep the reader moving forward by arousing interest in what is to come.
7) Use words that are suitable to the subject and the reader.
8) Make the opening paragraph state or suggest the topics of the other paragraphs.
9) Watch paragraph transitions.
10) Try to tie in the closing paragraph with the first paragraph. Try to give the reader the feeling that

you've done what you set out to do.

11) Check and correct grammar—at least for the final draft.

    a)   Check any doubtful spellings.

    b)   Check agreements between subjects and verbs.

    c)   Check for sentence fragments.

    d)   Check for comma splices.

    e)   Check tenses of verbs.

    f)   Check use of commas, semicolons, and quotation marks.

12) Try to make your writing sound smooth when read aloud.

13) Write or type the final draft very neatly.

I was satisfied with every point on my check list except the eighth. It's often a good idea to break a theme topic into three or four sub-topics, mention each sub-topic in the opening paragraph, and then develop each one in a separate paragraph. But I felt that, in this case, I'd handled my theme better than if I had followed Rule 8 closely.

After making a careful final draft, then, there was nothing to do but mail it, get busy on other lessons, and hope for the best as I waited to find out what my correspondence teacher thought of my efforts.

When my theme came back in the mail, I could scarcely wait to tear open the envelope. As soon as I looked at the top of the first page, I smiled from ear to ear and decided I had a really nice, intelligent teacher. She'd given me an *A* and had written on the theme: "Very nice indeed. Shows real ability, taste, and discrimination in the use of words. Pleasant style, too." (Notice those sentence fragments!) I thought maybe Webster and Roget deserved a little of the credit. But I wasn't complaining!

Now I was completely convinced that my teacher had had a good reason for saying, "Be more sensuous than Gissing if possible." I had to admit to myself that nothing I'd ever done before had proved to me so thoroughly the importance of using

13

words referring to things you could see, hear, feel, taste, or smell.

I had also figured out a way of thinking through a personal-experience theme. But I hadn't learned much from this lesson about writing the standard theme, the kind you can knock off in thirty or forty minutes and still have a well-organized and a well-written theme.

I'll tell you about this standard form in the next chapter.

CHAPTER 2

THE STANDARD THEME FORM
and
The In-Class Theme

"What is the best approach to writing an in-class theme?" This question has been asked by dozens of freshmen coming to my study for tutoring.

I am not sure that I know *the* best approach. But I do admit to them that I know a pretty good one.

When you have to compose a two-hundred to three-hundred-word theme in forty-five minutes, you don't have much time to write an outline, pencil off a first draft, and then write neatly and correctly a polished little masterpiece. To do decent in-class themes, .week after week, you must have a plan of attack that avoids the need for an elaborate outline or a second draft.

The approach that I'm suggesting is one that I've used myself, have taught, and have had consistently good reports on from students who have learned to use it. It's so simple that I'm surprised that English handbooks don't emphasize it a lot more than they do.

First, spend four or five minutes considering the subject or subjects that the teacher has assigned. After you've chosen the one that you feel you can write about most effectively, decide on three or four ways to look at the subject, and jot down these ideas. That is all the outline you need.

Then, somewhere in your opening paragraph, mention each of the three or four sub-topics you've decided upon. In the body of your theme, devote a paragraph to each of the sub-topics, using details and particulars, comparison or contrast, definition, examples, or any other method of paragraph development that suits the sub-topic. With the body of the theme completed, write a concluding paragraph that summarizes, looks to the future of the subject, or in some other way ties in with the opening paragraph.

It's a good idea not to wait until you have to do in-class themes to practice this approach to theme writing. One of the best times to practice this approach is when you have to write out-of-class themes, for the approach is equally useful for them.

Thanks to Jim, one of my students, I can show you exactly what I'm talking about. After Jim got back one of his better themes, he went over it with me, telling me how he went about composing it.

Jim had to write a theme on Hemingway's short story "The Killers." After reading the story a couple of times, he decided to write his theme on the reactions of three of the main characters to the "killers." Having decided on his topic, he reread the story marking statements and descriptions about the reactions of the three main characters.

Let's look at the way Jim developed his theme, which he kindly let me use as an example for other students. We'll examine it by the same method used to consider my theme in the first chapter.

An Explanation of "The Killers"

In "The Killers," Ernest Hemingway reveals man's

callous disregard for other people by observing the reactions of Sam, George, and Nick when they learn that an acquaintance is about to be murdered *[here in the opening sentence he gives his theme topic]*. Each of the three men learns about the murder plot when the killers wait to shoot Ole Andreson *[this identifies the acquaintance and gets the theme moving]* in a roadside diner *[tells place]*. Each man—Sam, the Negro cook *[further identification; the teacher has read the story, of course, but Jim gives enough information to make his discussion clear even to someone who hasn't]*; George, another employee of the diner; and Nick, a young man—must decide what courses of action to take.

Note that Jim has set up this opening paragraph so that he can devote a subsequent paragraph to the reaction of each man.

Sam thinks the best course of action is to avoid the situation *[a brief but effective topic sentence]*. His only statement to the killers is "Yes, Sir." His reaction expressed to George and Nick is "I don't like it. I don't like it at all." *[Almost invariably teachers like a student to support his statements with quotations from the story.]* When George suggests that Nick warn Ole, Sam says, "Mixing up in this ain't going to get you anywhere."

Of course, Jim doesn't use all the quotations that reveal Sam's reactions to the killers. He gives just enough to support his topic sentence adequately. The words in the paragraph come to sixty, and five paragraphs averaging sixty words each add up to exactly enough for a three-hundred-word theme.

George talks to the killers mainly to show them he is willing to do what they say. But his curiosity gets the better of him *[note the contrast to the topic sentence]* and he asks, "What are you going to kill Ole Andreson for?" As if in attempt to persuade them not to kill Ole, he asks, "What did he ever do to you?" George, however, has no intention of trying to become a hero, but he is willing for Nick to warn Ole.

17

Young Nick *[excellent transition here]* is evidently the least experienced of the three men in man's injustice to man *[topic sentence]*. He goes to warn Ole *[fact from story]*, even at the risk of personal harm. He discovers that Ole, who admits, "There ain't anything to do. . . .I got in wrong," has no hope of escaping the killers *[this sentence is a little awkward but contains good support for the statement of Ole's lack of hope]*. And thus Nick is terribly frustrated in his attempt to prevent an injustice. In the end, he has become much more like Sam and George *[Jim's own interpretation]*. He has come closer to accepting injustice.

In each of the three paragraphs of the body of the theme, Jim uses a generalization of his own as a topic sentence. Then he supports the generalization with a quotation or fact, or both, from the story.

In the concluding paragraph, Jim gives more of his own reactions. As he does in the beginning paragraph, he works in all three characters—Sam, George, and Nick—but in reverse order as if he were retracing his way back to the opening paragraph.

"The Killers" is a demonstration of how man becomes inured *[he found this word as a fitting synonym for "hardened"]* to injustice. Before young Nick sees Ole, he believes he can save the ex-fighter *[an additional detail from the story]* by warning him of the plot. George is still hoping to see a possible injustice prevented—by someone else *[summary of third paragraph]*. But Sam, whose color no doubt helped to accustom him to brutality *[Jim's own opinion]*, strongly advises Nick not to risk getting mixed up in the plot *[summary of second paragraph]*. Sam is a passive citizen who believes fighting injustice can bring only trouble *[this is a kind of personal reaction that teachers like—if the student supports it with facts or a quotation from the story as Jim does]*. Nick is frustrated in his attempt to help Ole. He has learned how not to right an injustice—by running away from it or by forgetting it

The Standard Theme Form

[this statement shows that Jim has reached a conclusion that he can apply to his own life; and, contrary to some students' opinions, most teachers do want you to relate what you learn to your own life!].

Don't you think you could write something about as good or better? Jim's theme is no world-shaking masterpiece, but it's well-organized, straightforward, and competent—competent enough, in fact, to get an *A-* and this comment from a rather strict teacher: "Very good content, expression, and mechanics."

This, then, is the standard form I spoke of: an opening paragraph with mention or suggestion of three or four sub-topics; a single paragraph developing each sub-topic; and a concluding paragraph. By writing five paragraphs, Jim comes out with just about four hundred words, right in the middle of the assigned length, between three hundred and five hundred words.

Richard, another of my students, decided to use the "standard form" for a theme he had to write about a group of poems. After deciding on the approach, he arranged four poems in the order of their success in achieving what he thought each poet set out to achieve. Here is the beginning of Richard's theme, entitled "Poetic Effectiveness."

William Blake's "London," William Wordsworth's "London, 1802," Matthew Arnold's "West London," and Stephen Spender's "An Elementary School Classroom in a Slum" all deal with the degradation that London suffered during the era of the Industrial Revolution *[gives theme topic and mentions all four poems]*. Each poet, in his own way, enters a plea for help from any reader capable of rendering assistance *[this sentence, like the first, states a characteristic that is common to all four poems]*.

This is a straightforward opening paragraph with few frills. But it does what the opening of a "standard" theme must do: It mentions the sub-topics, in this case the poems, that each of the paragraphs of the body of the theme discusses.

How to Study and Like It

Perhaps the best of these is the Matthew Arnold poem *[notice the use of the word "perhaps" in case the teacher might think another is best]*, because he does not simply paint a picture of wretchedness, but gives a simple dignity and honor to his characters *[support for his statement]*. He does not present a wide picture of depraved London, but narrows his scope to an example of two main characters, using them as a symbol of the broader view. *[Arnold and my student both realize that we are more interested in individual persons than we are in mankind as a whole.]* And in this fashion he gets across his point much more effectively than do the other three poets.

This paragraph has what most teachers look for in themes and essays. It has a generalization, that Arnold's poem is perhaps best, and it has reasons and details to support the generalization.

Stephen Spender's poem is possibly the second most effective with its portrayal of an elementary classroom in a London slum district *[topic sentence and generalization]*. Strongly stressing "equality of opportunity," he explains how the children's poor environment tends to lead them to the pathway of crime and delinquency *[here Richard tells what the poem does first]*. After stressing the piteousness of the slums, he enters a plea to "governor, teacher, inspector (or) visitor" to do something to give London's youth a chance to better themselves *[this sentence contains a bit of quoted material that English teachers seem to like so well]*. The poem seems to exaggerate the misery of the slums and to ignore any dignity that the children may have in spite of their living conditions *[here we have the reason for Richard's placing the poem second to Arnold's]*. The preaching in the poem is too obvious for maximum effectiveness *[Richard's opinion supported by the preceding sentence.]*

In this paragraph Richard has made no direct comparison to the other poems he is discussing. But the comparison is strongly implied.

20

The Standard Theme Form

William Blake generalizes on London's condition, "every . . . cry," "every voice," and stresses the moral depths into which so many of London's citizens have been forced *[topic sentence, generalization]*. Unlike Spender *[note comparison]*, however, he enters no direct plea, but simply gives a panoramic view of London's slums. *[Richard places the poem third behind Arnold's and Spender's because he considers it too general.]*

William Wordsworth does not go into any great detail concerning London's plight, but seems only to praise Milton, a reformer of times past. He calls on Milton to do what he might very well be doing himself *[this is, no doubt, the reason Richard places the poem last in effectiveness]*. And the result is relative ineffectiveness *[generalization]*, neither inspiring the reader to action *[reason for generalization]* nor inspiring the reader to entertain sympathetic feelings for the poverty-stricken English during the Industrial Revolution.

Notice that the statements Richard makes about the poems in his theme all relate to what the poem does, what the poet *apparently* meant it to do, and how effectively the poem achieves what the poet was apparently trying to achieve. All three ways in which Richard considers each poem involve his judgments and opinions. But teachers do like to know that students have opinions—*provided that they give support for them from the materials they are considering.*

Perhaps with a little more effort Wordsworth could have surpassed Arnold's poem *[Richard's conclusion]*. Certainly these four poems have been vivid examples of the old adage, "It's what you do with what you've got that counts."

Notice that the concluding paragraph contains a reference to the sub-topics, the four poems, that the entire theme deals with. It's not an exceptionally good conclusion, but it follows the standard form. Using a quotation or old saying in the concluding sentence is often an effective device.

The conclusion is the most important part of the theme, mainly because it's normally the last part a teacher reads. For most writing, however, the beginning is the most important part, because you have to grab the interest of your reader in the beginning and make him want to read on, or he will never get to the conclusion.

A good way to get ideas for writing conclusions is to study the last paragraphs of articles in such magazines as *Scientific American* and *Reader's Digest.* You might also study the beginning paragraphs, but if you do, keep in mind that the theme is really a different form of writing from the magazine article.

"Why, then," you might ask, "are students required to write the three-hundred to five-hundred-word theme?" One reason is that you don't have time to write much more than that in a fifty- or sixty-minute class period. Many freshmen I've known didn't feel that they could write that much and do a decent job of it. But that was before they learned the "standard" theme form.

The standard theme form enables you to organize your theme quickly. It is also flexible. If your teacher favors long themes, you can take the same basic organizational plan and vary the length of the theme by the amount of development you give each paragraph. The paragraphs don't need to be the same length. One of your sub-topics may be considerably more important than the others. You can emphasize it more by developing its paragraph in greater detail.

Why am I putting so much emphasis on the standard form when I have said there are other good approaches? Mainly because you can always use it and be assured of a well-organized theme. If you know how you are going to organize your theme, you can develop the paragraphs more easily and have more time to check your sentence mechanics.

With a little practice in writing the standard theme, you will become more aware of the structure of magazine articles, of short stories, and of chapters in books. In fact, in the next chapter we are going to consider a magazine article in order to develop another important method of improving your writing. The method is called *reading for technique.*

Right now, though, let's list the steps for writing the standard theme:

1) Choose your subject carefully (if you have a choice),
2) Divide your subject into three or four sub-topics,
3) Mention your sub-topics in your opening paragraph,
4) Develop each sub-topic in a separate paragraph by the most effective means you can think of,
5) Write a conclusion referring to your sub-topics.

The next time you find yourself staring at a blank sheet of paper trying to think of a way to approach your theme topic, remember the standard theme form. It is a good approach to think of first, and one you can always use if you cannot think of one you like better.

SUGGESTION FOR FURTHER STUDY: *The Elements of Style,* by William Strunk, Jr. and E. B. White, available in a Macmillan paperback, is a brief, excellent little book that treats mechanics, composition, and style.

CHAPTER 3

READING TO WRITE
and
The Character-Sketch Theme

"How do you go about writing a character sketch?" asked Linda, a tall, pretty freshman I was tutoring twice a week one semester.

I thought for a moment and looked at Linda, but I didn't answer her question. "Linda," I said, "do you know what I think would be the best way to start preparing for your character sketch?"

"No," she said. "What is it?"

"I think you should start by looking for some of the secrets a good writer uses in a character sketch," I replied. I'd heard and read of the usual ways of characterization—by showing a character in action, by quoting him and telling how he speaks, by showing his reactions to other people and things, by showing other characters' reactions to him, and so on. But instead of just telling Linda, I thought it might be a lot more effective if she considered a piece of writing that used the various devices of characterization.

"Where in the world do you find such secrets?" she asked, looking a little puzzled.

"Don't you know where all writers reveal their best writing secrets?" I asked.

"Heavens no!" she exclaimed. "If I did, I wouldn't need to ask you about writing a character sketch." I nodded my head in agreement, and she smiled.

"I've heard and read that writers reveal their best secrets and techniques in their published writings," I pointed out, *"if you know how to look for them."*

"I thought there must be a catch to it somewhere," she said with a frown. "You were making it sound too easy. Besides, I don't want to be an author."

"But don't you have to be an author of letters, themes, and essay exams?" I asked. "And you do want to learn about writing in the way that's easiest and most fun, don't you?"

"Of course." She nodded, but she still didn't seem convinced.

"Then you want to learn to read for technique," I said. "That is, you want to read to write."

"I've read a lot of books just for enjoyment, but I don't remember finding any writing secrets in what I read," Linda answered, frowning dubiously.

"I dare say you've absorbed a few of the secrets unconsciously. But you can do much better than that," I said.

"How?" she asked, turning her head slightly to one side.

"By turning around."

"Now what in the world do you mean?" she interrupted.

"Let me explain," I said. "Nearly all students have learned to read for only one reason—for the information and the emotional kick the authors can get across."

Linda sighed and looked puzzled. "Isn't that the way I'm supposed to read?"

"Well, that's the way the author wants you to read," I agreed. "But as long as you do read that way you're almost totally unaware of *how* he is conveying information to you and *how* he is giving you an emotional kick."

"What does that have to do with 'turning around'?" Linda asked.

"Just a moment, and you'll see," I promised. "For a few lines, now, read along in your regular way, except this time try to be even more aware than usual of the information the author is getting across to you. And pay even more attention than usual to your own emotional response to the piece of writing. Then stop, and turn your point of view around. This time, don't consider the author's *solutions* to his writing problems, as you usually do. Instead, try to consider what his *problems* were and *how* he solved them."

She began to smile. "I think I get the idea," she said, nodding. "What kinds of questions should I ask myself?"

"What was his problem to begin with?" I caught my breath and hurried on. "What kind of information did he want to get across? What kind of reader did he probably have in mind? What kind of emotional response did he want from his reader? *How* does he succeed in getting across the information and emotional impact he does?"

"Let me jot them down," she said, opening a notebook.

I repeated the questions for her. "In other words," I continued, "instead of focusing altogether on the product of the author's efforts, you speculate on the materials and goals he had to begin with."

"Yes, but what are the advantages of considering the author's problems?" Linda asked.

"You gain in two ways from this kind of effort," I told her. "First, by speculating about the author's problems, you will learn to ask useful questions about your *own* writing problems. The first step toward solving any problem is to recognize what the problem is. Second, you will find that you can apply some of the author's solutions to your own writing problems."

"I've never considered doing it before," she said, looking thoughtful. "But it does sound like an interesting idea. You wouldn't advise me to read that way all the time, would you?"

I shook my head. "Not unless you were a professional writer. And even if you were, I doubt that you'd want to read for technique all the time."

"When should I read for technique, then?" Linda asked, ready to jot my answer down.

"When you have a specific problem as you do now, or when you read something you like particularly well, or whenever a piece of writing strikes you as well done and you want to take time to learn from it," I replied, preparing to go look for a character sketch.

I remembered reading recently a character sketch in *Reader's Digest* that I'd particularly liked. It dealt with an old gaucho in Argentina, a man of such freedom, skill, self-reliance, and individuality that I thought both girls and boys would enjoy examining how his character was developed in the sketch.

After I located the issue I wanted from a stack of magazines, I flipped to "The Most Unforgettable Character I've Met," by George Obligado (*Reader's Digest,* February 1963, pp. 115-20). After rereading the article and discussing it with Linda, I decided it would serve as an interesting example of characterization to include here.

But first let's clarify what characterization means. How do you describe another person? It almost always seems more difficult to characterize persons we know well than to describe mere acquaintances or even strangers. That may be why George Obligado wrote a sketch about an Argentine gaucho instead of a neighbor he might have known much better. Perhaps we don't like to talk about the people we know best. Or maybe it's too difficult to select the most revealing traits from so many that we are familiar with.

Although it's impossible to know anyone completely, we do form opinions of people. A person's actions are probably the most basic source of opinions. There's an old saying that "actions speak louder than words." A person also reveals his character by what he says and how he says it, as well as by the effect he has on other people, and by the way he reacts to them in terms of his actions and words.

Taking these ways of knowing a person together with objective descriptions about how he looks, his occupation, and so on, and what he thinks, we have almost all the methods of characterization that a writer of fiction uses. Usually the writer of fiction lets us know what one or more of the sympathetic characters thinks, but he doesn't let us know what goes on in the minds of his villains. If we understand how a person thinks and why he acts as he does, we may feel sorry for him or we may like him, but we probably won't hate him.

The writer who deals with real people is unable to develop his characters by telling what a person thinks if he does not say it or show it in his actions. Playwrights and writers of television and movie scripts cannot use this method either.

But all the other methods of characterization are available to them and to the writer of a character sketch. They can show us the character of a person and tell us what they please about the occupation, appearance, sex, and other features of the subject.

To write a satisfactory character sketch, however, a writer must do more than merely use the devices of characterization. He must arouse our interest at the beginning, maintain it through the middle, and at the end leave us with the feeling that we have been acquainted with a person worth knowing.

Now let's look at selections from George Obligado's character sketch to see how he attracts and maintains our interest and how he uses some of the devices of characterization. We'll examine these passages in the same way we looked at the themes in the two previous chapters. Only the point of view is changed in that neither you nor I is acquainted with this author, whose sketch begins:

I was throwing a ball against the side of our barn *[characterizes narrator as a young boy and locates the action in the country]* when I heard the sound of an

28

automobile *[both visual and auditory images in the first sentence].* Cars were not common where we lived in Argentina 40 years ago *[establishes the country and the time]*—our *estancia* was 100 miles northwest of Buenos Aires—so I ran toward the road *[gets movement into the account].* A strange contraption came through our gate *[arouses curiosity].* It was a Model T Ford, but it had no body and no seats *[notice point of view: the boy was likely to notice the automobile before its driver].* The driver, a gaucho *[occupation],* was riding comfortably on a saddle secured to a gas tank. A short, heavy whip hung from his right wrist *[one of the many effective visual images],* as if he intended to use it on the jalopy. His possessions rode behind him in a bundle roped to a board bolted to the chassis *[characterization by description of possessions].* On top of everything was his guitar.

In going through this opening paragraph we have commented on several of Obligado's phrases and sentences, which serve as solutions to his writing problems. Now let's imagine what problems they are solving. Like all writers, Obligado has to grab our interest and establish the point of view. And in this paragraph he also has to introduce the main character.

How does he grab our interest? He does it by appealing to our senses of sight and sound. He shows himself in an easily *visualized* situation—a boy is tossing a ball against a barn—and then he introduces the *sound* of an automobile. Because the sound of a car would not in itself arouse much curiosity; he quickly points out that it was unusual when he was a boy.

While attracting our interest, he establishes the point of view, that of the first-person narrator. In the second sentence he locates the scene in space and time and directs our attention toward the main character. In the third sentence he increases our curiosity about the car. Then he begins the characterization by describing the car and its driver. As you see, once you become aware of *what* the author is doing, it is fairly easy to imagine the problem he is solving. The sketch continues:

> When he saw me he stopped. "Is your father around?" he asked.
>
> "He'll probably be in the garden."
>
> "Please take me to him."

At ten, it was my pride never to obey an order without arguing *[characterization of author by telling]*, but from that man emanated a calm authority that could not be ignored *[characterization by reaction of narrator to character]*. I led him to our garden, where my father was showing a peon how to couple some water pipes.

"Good morning, *señor*," the newcomer said. "My name is Patricio O'Connell. I was born near here; my father was overseer of the neighboring estate *[characterization by direct quotation]*. Now I come from the Andes region. I wonder if you have some little job for me? I do many things well."

My father studied the hawklike face, whose predatory features were tempered by a rosy complexion that sun, rain and wind had not altered, and by green, dreamy eyes *[a clever way to introduce a physical description of the gaucho]*. A man of about 50 *[characterization by age]*, the gaucho wore typical cowboy attire: short black jacket, ample trousers tucked into medium-high boots, wide leather belt ornamented with silver coins, and a soft hat disdainfully tilted backward *[characterization by description of clothing]*. "No, Patricio," my father said. "I have nothing at the moment."

The stranger did not seem to mind. He looked cheerfully around *[characterization by reaction to a situation]*. "May I ask why you are putting these pipes together?"

My father replied, "I am building a little fountain. The water brought by these pipes will emerge through a few stones, and it will look like a natural spring."

"But it won't *be* natural," Patricio said *[characterization by reaction]*.

"You won't find a spring within a hundred miles, man!" said my father.

"I think I can find a spring for you." Patricio took a spade from the hands of a startled peon *[characterization by action of Patricio, reaction of peon]*. "Follow me, señor, please."

We followed Patricio *[characterization by reaction of other characters]* to the end of the garden and halfway down the wooded cliff beyond it, to an open shelf that was shaded by a spreading ceibo tree. Patricio carefully inspected the bank beneath the tree *[characterization by action of main character]*. At a certain point he made a hole with the spade, and a narrow streak of water trickled out.

"I discovered this spring when I hunted otters here as a boy," Patricio explained. "In a few days' time I could make you a nice little fountain."

"There are no quarters for you," my father protested feebly *[characterization by reaction]*.

"It doesn't matter. I'll build myself a hut, and a lean-to for my car *[characterization by reaction]*."

"I thought you came on horseback," said my father, pointing to the gaucho's whip.

"This? Oh, it comes in handy in case there's a fight. I don't like to use a knife *[characterization by character's own statement]*."

"Very well, you may stay—but only until you finish the fountain *[characterization by reaction]*."

"I wouldn't stay a day longer," Patricio answered proudly. "I like to roam." Then, turning to me, he said, "I need some wire for my hut. Will you come with me to the store?" He placed me beside him on the gas tank *[characterization by action]*, and we drove off in what

31

seemed to me the most glamorous car in Argentina.

As you can see, these paragraphs of the character sketch are so skillfully tied together, and the forward movement is so well paced, that it is difficult for us to stop and ask ourselves just what the author has done. Apparently in this scene between the gaucho and the author's father, the author has set out to reveal one side of the gaucho's resourcefulness. The author has kept up our interest by creating a conflict between the father, who doesn't want the gaucho to stay, and the gaucho himself, who wants to stay and make himself useful. Before the conflict is resolved, the author whets our curiosity by presenting the gaucho's whip a second time, and you know now that he prefers the whip to a knife. Why? You want to read on to find out:

"What happened to the body?" I asked. "Did you crash?"

"No, but a friend did. The body of his car was ruined, so I took mine off and gave it to him *[characterization by reaction shown in a quotation]*. He had a family, you see."

Several horses waited in the dust in front of the country store, a place where a man could buy everything from a tractor to a lady's hat, and then get drunk to forget how much he had spent. My father usually made me wait outside, but now I walked in proudly with Patricio *[characterization by reaction of narrator]*. After he bought the wire, he ordered two orangeades.

A fat man lounging at the bar laughed derisively *[characterization by reaction of another character]*. "Orangeade? A big fellow like you? Have a gin with me!"

"No, thanks, *amigo*. Another day" *[characterization by reaction of main character]*.

"No man has ever refused to drink with me!" the man said angrily.

"Well, now one has. It's hot in here, isn't it?" Patricio rolled up his left sleeve, revealing the scars of many knife wounds across his sunburnt arm *[characterization by action]*. The fat man swore, threw a coin on the counter,

32

and left quickly *[characterization by reaction of a secondary character]*.

Later I learned that in his youth Patricio had been famous for his hot temper and his skill as a fighter *[characterization by telling, but effective here]*. Once, however, his knife had seriously wounded a man. Although the judge decided that he had acted in self-defense, from that moment he gave up drinking and fighting *[characterization by reaction]*. If things grew dangerous, he would grab his heavy whip by the lash and use it to disarm his adversary.

It is easy to see what the author is doing. He is presenting a character who not only is superior in fighting skills but knows his own abilities and weaknesses and elects to keep them always under control. The author not only *tells* us but *shows* us, and here he shows us first.

Obligado presents other episodes in detail, showing the gaucho's resourcefulness in constructing his hut and his skill in breaking a wild horse. He shows him singing his gaucho songs at night as he strums his guitar. There seems to be no end to the practical skills Patricio has mastered. The author chooses to move into the final episode with a paragraph telling of his accomplishments:

It was autumn before Patricio's fountain was finished. This was not his fault. There was always something else that needed doing. A storm wrecked the windmill and blew away the tiles from the barn roof. A bull broke the wire fence. Our boat leaked. The kitchen chimney needed cleaning *[notice the specific details]*. Patricio attended to all these minor emergencies *[characterization by reaction to situations]*. But at last the fountain was finished. . . .

To celebrate the completion 30 neighbors *[a specific number that makes the account more believable]* were invited, and benches and tables were set under the ceibo tree. Patricio was in charge of barbecuing the two lambs *[he seems to be able to do everything around a ranch!]*, and, after we had eaten and the red wine of the region had circulated freely, we looked to him for a song. He tuned his guitar and sang some stanzas of "Martin Fierro." . . . He ended with a song that filled me with foreboding *[characterization by reaction of narrator]*, for it sounded like a farewell.

Abruptly he rose and left *[suggests the decisiveness in his character]*. I wanted to run after him, but two old ladies kept me, trying to figure out from which grandparent I acquired my nose and eyes. *[Either this is a bit of fiction to make the sketch more vivid or else the author has an extraordinary memory.]* When I finally ran to my friend's hut, I could hear the Ford idling *[the same Ford that he heard at the beginning of the sketch]*. Patricio's possessions were already tied to the chassis in a bundle with the guitar on top. He was securing the girth of the saddle around the gas tank.

"Oh, Patricio, don't go, please!" I implored *[characterization by reaction of narrator]*, hanging onto his short black jacket.

"I must," he said. Then he added solemnly, "I have heard that 400 kilometers from here, in a place called Tandil, there is a big stone that weighs many tons and swings from side to side, but so slowly that to notice it you have to put a bottle under it." *[Probably this statement is meant to show Patricio's understanding of young boys and to show his response to challenges to his sense of adventure.]*

"Take me with you!"

He smiled fondly *[characterization by reaction]*. "You know I can't. But wait. I'll give you a souvenir." *[A decision.]*

He fumbled among his things and produced a grimy notebook filled with his clumsy writing, and handed it to me *[an act growing out of his decision]*. "These are my songs *[probably his most precious possession]*, the ones you like so much."

I could not thank him, for I was crying. He lifted me in his powerful arms and kissed me on the forehead *[characterization by gesture]*. Then he climbed onto the gas tank and drove off *[we have come full circle: he leaves as he came]*. I remained a long time watching the cloud of dust rising slowly over the plain."

In the final paragraph, the author tells us simply the kind of man he has shown us so effectively:

The other day I found that tattered notebook and recognized in those verses the artless efforts of an untutored but marvelously versatile man. Philosopher, teacher, poet, musician, horseman—Patricio was always ready to tread all paths that opened to him. He enjoyed participating in the boundless variety of this world. He knew that life is as broad and beautiful as the pampa itself, and he planted this lesson in the heart of a little boy who now, as a man, in another country and another way of life, remembers him gratefully.

Even with parts of the sketch left out, no doubt you sense some of the reasons this sketch was selected from among hundreds of others for inclusion in *Reader's Digest.* But you may be wondering why the sketch of an unknown gaucho was chosen over sketches of well-known Americans. You may be wondering, too, why I selected the sketch to illustrate some of the devices of characterization. The editors of *Reader's Digest* may have included it for the same reason I have used it.

In an age of specialization and dependence on passive entertainment, it is good to know about a kind, versatile, self-reliant man like Patricio O'Connell and to realize that college students, as well as a ten-year-old boy, can respond warmly to such a man.

From considering both the methods and the results of what George Obligado has done, you can get ideas about learning to read for technique and about writing character sketches.

If you do write a character sketch, I hope you will do as well as Linda, the first student with whom I discussed the sketch of Patricio O'Connell. After we went through the piece carefully, sentence by sentence, she talked about various people she might use as subjects, and then decided to write a sketch of her father. She knew that it was harder to write about someone in her immediate family than about a distant acquaintance, but she was willing to tackle the harder problem.

Before the end of the tutorial session she made a list of the main characterization devices and scribbled a few points under each that would apply to her father, a small-town banker. Here are the devices she listed:

Characterization by Showing
(the most effective kind)

1) Showing character in action (including gestures)
2) Showing him speaking
3) Showing his reaction to other characters, things, ideas
4) Showing other characters' reactions to him

Characterization by Telling

1) Telling what a character looks like
2) Telling his age, occupation, national origin
3) Telling his traits and motives

About a week and a half later, Linda was smiling cheerfully when she arrived for her tutorial session. "I've got something for you to read," she said, handing me her entire theme except the last page. "You have to guess what grade I made on it," she said, beaming.

In the very first paragraph she showed her father in his bank office, his feet propped up on a desk, as he smoked a cigar and read farm magazines and *The Wall Street Journal* before it was time for the bank to open. In another paragraph she had a farmer asking for and receiving a loan to tide him over until harvest. She showed a good deal of her father's character in his reaction to the farmer and in the farmer's reaction to him. In short, it was a warm, believable portrait of a well-liked, small-town banker.

I noticed that almost no grammatical or spelling errors were marked. Although grading any theme or essay answer is a highly subjective process, I thought I recognized an *A* theme, by almost any teacher's standards. "This looks better than a *C*," I teased, reaching for the last page of the theme.

Disappointment at my comment showed on Linda's face. "No," I said, "I'm afraid if I were grading it, I'd have to give you an *A*. I'll bet you got at least an *A-*."

She looked much happier now as she let me see the first *A* her teacher had given her—along with the comment, "Well done."

When Linda's grades were nearly all *A's* at the end of the semester, including an *A* in English, we were both thankful to George Obligado. I was very glad I'd chosen a sketch about an Argentine gaucho to teach her about reading to write.

CHAPTER 4

READING TO KNOW AND ENJOY:
The Magic of Black Ink and White Paper

When I hear someone mention rapid reading, I am reminded of a conversation I overheard at a football game.

"What happened? What happened? Who has the ball?" a cute blonde shouted to her boyfriend over the roar of the crowd at Owen Stadium.

As soon as the noise of the crowd had quieted down and he had caught his breath from cheering, the boyfriend explained to her as only an ex-football player or sports announcer could. "First our quarterback faked a handoff to his left halfback. Then he whirled, faked a lateral to his right half, and handed the ball to his fullback going up the middle."

He caught his breath and hurried on. "Their center linebacker forced our fullback to fumble. Their left linebacker recovered the fumble, but before he could get good possession of the ball our right tackle hit him and forced a fumble. Then our quarterback caught the ball in the air and dived for a nine-yard gain before he could be stopped!"

"My goodness!" the blonde murmurred, impressed. "How did you see all that?"

"Oh, I don't know," he said with a grin. "I guess when you've played football since you were eight or nine years old, you learn what to look for and you see it quickly."

'Ohhh," she sighed, shaking her head with admiration, still not convinced that her boyfriend didn't have some kind of extraordinary visual ability. Like many football fans, she just tried to follow the ball and missed seeing most of the play in the line and down field.

She reminded me of people who read only a word at a time and don't shift their focus from point to point very quickly.

The boyfriend had learned to watch a football game somewhat like the way a lot of good readers read. Even though his eyes focused on the quarterback, he was aware of the moves of the halfbacks and the center linemen, and he shifted his focus rapidly enough to grasp most of the action in detail.

Similarly, rapid readers usually grasp three or more words at a time and shift their sight quickly and often. Having read a great deal and partly knowing what to expect, they can read and move on with great speed to grasp both what is said and the way it's tied together.

That's the kind of reading we're talking about in this chapter. It's not study; we'll go into that later. It's a process of pushing forward through the printed words as rapidly as your eyes and mind will allow. It's an attempt to get an impression of a story or novel or text *as a whole.*

For example, a rapid reader might read the third paragraph of this chapter by making the following fixations or focuses:

As soon as / the noise / of the crowd / quieted down / and he caught / his breath / from yelling, / the boyfriend / explained to her / as only / an ex-football player / or sports announcer / could. / "First our quarterback / faked a handoff / to his left halfback. / Then he whirled, / faked a lateral / to his right half, / and handed the ball / to his

fullback / going up the middle." / The boyfriend / caught
his breath / and hurried on. /

The goal of rapid reading is to see a work in its entirety, to
get a feeling for how the pieces fit together. Depending on your
earlier experiences with the ideas, the images, and the
vocabulary, your first impression of a work may be cloudy in
some places, clear and sharp in others. You can focus on the
obscure parts later as you study.

The kind of reading we're talking about is not done with the
nagging thought, "I must remember this." It's the kind of
reading, usually rapid, intended to generate the feeling, "Isn't
this interesting to know? Isn't it amazing how everything ties
together?"

This kind of reading requires desire, skill, and a sense of awe
before the magic of the written word. The desire may come
from knowing that the study time you devote to rapid reading
is time extremely well spent. The skill comes from knowledge
of techniques and from practice. The sense of awe? That comes
from reflecting on what an extraordinary process reading truly
is.

Do you remember the joy you felt when you first began to
read? You thought, no doubt, that it was a big step toward the
world of adults. One of my earliest memories is of my brother's
reading to me a cartoon strip. He didn't like to do it very often.
So I felt very grown up the first time I found I could read the
strip. I strutted up to my brother and asked him to read it to
me. When he refused, I proudly showed him that I could read it
for myself.

I am afraid that learning to read doesn't give quite as much
delight to people who spent much of their time in front of a
television set as they were growing up. But even for them,
reading is often more satisfying than watching television or the
movies. As their reading skill improves, a sense of power
develops from being able to transform the black marks on white
paper into meaningful words that relate to their experiences.

In this sense, reading is meaningful basically in terms of the way you see, hear, feel, smell, and taste. If you've never taken time to watch a colorful sunset, words describing the slowly changing pinks, yellows, and reds may at first be lost upon you. But the description of the colors and the flow of the words describing them may well make you eager to experience more deeply the beauty of a sunset the next time you have a chance.

Reading, then, serves two basic functions. First, it appeals to your previous experiences, both those having to do with sense perceptions and those of earlier reading, and it helps organize those experiences in new and interesting ways. Second, it helps prepare you to perceive life around you more intensely and to respond to it more actively and meaningfully.

"Words are power," the ancients said. Saint John went further: "In the beginning was the Word, and the Word was with God, and the Word was God." No doubt the words of Saint John, of Plato, and of Aristotle have affected more people than all the deeds of Alexander the Great. And what British monarch has touched as many lives as Shakespeare?

In many societies, reading and writing were jealously guarded secrets of the priestly ruling class. The rest of the people looked with awe upon those blessed enough by the gods to be able to read.

Reading and writing made it possible to preserve with little change the wisdom and experience that had been transmitted before only in the spoken words handed down from generation to generation. It isn't surprising that much of the earliest writing was considered sacred.

Nor is it surprising that man has come to dominate the earth only since he has learned to read and write. That is, only since he has learned to express his thoughts and feelings both in sounds and in the visual symbols for these sounds, written words. The word is the boundary between man and animal. And we can say not only that writing began history but that written words are the flesh of history and of civilization as well.

Truly the written word is a marvelous thing. With the written word man began to be able to think abstractly and to use the principle of transformation and inversion of symbols. For example, the written word to the beginning pupil is only a symbol for a sound, which is a symbol for a thing or an action. C-a-t is the symbol for the sound "cat," which suggests one of all the furry, purry little animals the child has known. Twenty or thirty years later, after the child has grown up, he may think of the "catty" woman next door when he hears the word "cat."

It's little wonder that many children who are developing reading skills at a satisfactory pace often prefer reading to watching television. Reading allows them to proceed as rapidly as their reading speed will allow, as well as to tie the written words to their experience as they will. Reading is more creative and imaginative than the mere watching of television or movies.

For you, too, reading can be an amazing process over which you exercise a great deal of control. You may be able to read three short stories with good understanding and appreciation in the time you could watch the dramatization of only one on television. You can learn to read very rapidly, skimming along, when you are concerned with getting only a broad, not very detailed, perspective on what you are reading. At other times you may want to read slowly, letting the beauty of a descriptive passage appeal vividly to your senses. Sometimes you may find a passage so striking that you want to read it aloud. Certainly almost all poetry should be read aloud.

Unfortunately, if you are like most students, you need to improve your reading skills. Fortunately, if you are like most students, you have a great deal of potential for improvement. There are two ways to improve your reading skill, and they reinforce each other. One way is to improve your physical reading habits. The other way is to improve your vocabulary.

One bad reading habit that slows students down is the habit of moving the lips while reading. This habit keeps you from reading much faster than you can talk. The cure is simple. When you catch yourself moving your lips as you read, hold a hand over your lips for a while. Students who can rid themselves of this habit often double their reading speed within days.

Another excellent way to increase reading speed is by reading just for the subjects and verbs. In most writing, these words carry most of the meaning. As someone has said, the rest is mainly window dressing.

Of course, when you read for subjects and verbs, many of the other words will also register in your mind. But the most meaningful parts of the sentence will stand out the most clearly. You will also develop a certain rhythm to your reading, with subjects and verbs providing the beat. For example, you might read one of the opening paragraphs of this chapter this way:

Their center LINEBACKER FORCED our fullback to fumble. Their left LINEBACKER RECOVERED the fumble, but before HE COULD GET good possession of the ball, our right TACKLE HIT him and FORCED a fumble. Then our QUARTERBACK CAUGHT the ball in the air and DIVED for a nine-yard gain before HE COULD BE STOPPED.

Of course, if you start worrying too much about which words are the subjects and which are the verbs, you may find the technique slows you down at first. But by practicing the technique, you can improve both your speed and your comprehension.

Remember that a good reader varies his reading speed according to the material he is reading. For a novel or short story, you're better off reading quickly in order to get the motion and emotion. But for a book on math or physics, for example, you *have to* read slowly and analytically from the beginning. A rapid reading of a chapter of math may accomplish little or nothing.

A good reader learns to analyze his tendency to drop back a line or two and reread. Such regressions can have any one of three causes, and you can learn to distinguish them. The three main causes for regression in reading are difficult subject matter, poorly written material, and reader fatigue or lack of concentration.

Well written material has the subjects and verbs close

43

together in most sentences. Poorly written material may have two or three long phrases or clauses between the subject and the verb. By the time you get to the verb you may have forgotten the subject.

Well written material may be difficult to read because its subject matter is abstract and the terminology is unfamiliar.

Good textbooks define many of the terms likely to be unfamiliar, but you may still need to read with a dictionary and a notebook at your side.

If the terminology is familiar enough to you, and the subjects and verbs are reasonably close together, and you are still tending to regress, you may be tired or lacking in concentration. In that case, you need either to get some rest or to apply the study techniques discussed in a later chapter of this book.

Many colleges and universities have non-credit courses designed to increase students' reading speed and comprehension. Often both increase at the same time. In some schools the courses are given at very little cost. In one university, for example, the charge is only fourteen dollars for fourteen hours of instruction, including the use of films and machines. One machine, the tachistoscope, flashes up to six or seven words on a screen for only a fraction of a second. The student hasn't time to shift the focus of his eyes, yet he learns to grasp all the words. Such reading courses may greatly improve your reading habits. They are well worth your consideration—and your time and money.

In addition to improving your physical reading skills, another way to improve your reading ability is to increase your vocabulary. You learn most new words from reading, and you probably don't look many of them up in a dictionary.

The first time you see a new word, you get some idea of the meaning from the other words in the sentence. When you see it again in a slightly different context, you get a still better idea of its meaning. After you see it several times you gain a good grasp of the meaning. It becomes a part of your recognition vocabulary. After a while, you decide to use it in your writing or your speech. If you use it in your writing, you are probably wary enough of its meaning to check it in a dictionary. Once you have used a word a few times, it becomes a part of your active vocabulary. It's yours!

Perhaps you want a faster way to build your vocabulary. Fortunately, there are books of exercises intended to increase your vocabulary. In recent years I have used and examined a half dozen or so excellent ones. And I think the best of these is *Word Power Made Easy,* by Norman Lewis. Delightfully written, this book has a number of exercises that take you quickly through the normal processes of learning new words. First, Lewis exemplifies in a brief, entertaining paragraph the word he is about to introduce. For example:

This man's attitude to life is simple, direct, and aboveboard—every decision he makes is based on the answer to one question: "What is in it for me?" If his selfishness, greed, and ruthless desire for self-advancement hurts other people, that's too bad. "This is a tough world, pal, dog eat dog, every man for himself, and I, for one, am not going to be left behind."

He's an egoist.

After introducing a dozen or so related words, Lewis gives brief exercises that make the words a part of your recognition (or passive) vocabulary. In other exercises, he asks you to provide the proper words for the definitions he gives. Thus the words become a part of your active vocabulary.

Often Lewis explores the origins of words, breaking them down into the original Latin or Greek roots and showing how other words derive from the same roots. This inverts the objective way of looking at the words. It gets you on the "inside." Having two ways to look at them, you are more likely to remember them. Aware that *male-* means bad and *-factor* means "doer," you might guess that "malefactor" means an evil doer or criminal even if you'd never seen the word before. Looking at words from the inside, you become more conscious of the basic or root meanings of words. And you may become

45

eager to keep a notebook of words that you look up or words that you particularly like.

Lewis' *Word Power Made Easy* can be of exceptional value to you. I would estimate that each hour you spend studying the chapters of the book and working methodically through the exercises will add more to your vocabulary than fifteen or twenty hours of reading good novels. I recommend it without reservation.

Another vocabulary book almost as good is *How to Build a Better Vocabulary*, by Maxwell Nurnberg and Morris Rosenblum. Like *Word Power Made Easy*, it is available in paperback. This book puts even more emphasis on word origins. It too has numerous exercises to help make the words a part of your vocabulary. You can have fun building your vocabulary with either book, or both.

Still another way of improving your vocabulary is to do the vocabulary quiz called "Word Power" in *Reader's Digest* each month. With this alone you can review or learn twenty words each month.

As students increase their awareness of new words and their meanings, roots, and origins, they often learn to enjoy browsing in dictionaries, thesauruses, and dictionaries of synonyms. Of course, dictionaries give the words they define in alphabetical order. Thesauruses patterned after *Roget's Thesaurus* arrange related words together according to the idea expressed. Dictionaries of synonyms, such as *Webster's Dictionary of Synonyms*, explore the differences between the meanings of similar words and give examples of their usage.

All these ways of improving your vocabulary can improve your reading speed and comprehension. You tend to pause when you see an unfamiliar word, whether you look it up or not. Two or three unfamiliar words in a sentence can completely prevent your understanding the sentence.

Improving your vocabulary helps you in your writing and speaking, too, provided you exercise a little intelligence in deciding when it's appropriate to use the new words you have learned. Unless you want to be a show-off, you will use words to express your thoughts, not to impress your friends with the fact that you know some words they don't know.

Still another way of improving your reading is, strangely enough, learning to read in another language. Anyone who learns to read in and translate from a foreign language is sure to improve his vocabulary in his native language. We'll take up the study of foreign languages in the next chapter.

In summary:

A) Improve your reading skills.
   1) Make sure you don't lip read.
   2) Increase the number of words you can take in with each movement of the eyes.
   3) Avoid dropping back to reread.
   4) Try reading with emphasis on subjects and verbs.
   5) Vary your speed according to the material.
   6) Enroll in a speed-reading course at your school.
   7) Be aware that reading is a wonderful, magical process.

B) Improve your vocabulary.
   1) Read good books.
   2) Study *Word Power Made Easy* and *How to Build a Better Vocabulary.*
   3) Take the "Word Power" test in *Reader's Digest* each month.
   4) Use a good dictionary, paying particular attention to the origins of words and using the words you look up in brief sentences that you say to yourself.
   5) Use a thesaurus.
   6) Examine words in *Webster's Dictionary of Synonyms* or in an unabridged dictionary.
   7) Write in a notebook words that you look up and particularly like.
   8) Study a foreign language.

We have referred repeatedly to reading as a magical process. And *magical* is not too strong a word for the process of transforming black marks on white paper into the images and concepts by which we think and feel. Webster defines magic as the art that produces its effects by "a mastery of secret forces of nature."

Despite theories involving electrical impulses in the axons of brain and other nerve cells, no one claims to really understand the transformations of the printed word into visual images as varied as the hues of the rainbow; into images of touch as delicate as the fur of a coat rubbing against the hand or as painful as a throbbing tooth; into images of tastes as bitter as quinine and as sweet as honey; into images of smells as stinking as a skunk or as fragrant as Parisian perfume; into images of sounds as fearsome as the wail of a siren or as peaceful as the bells of a cathedral; into thoughts as crippling as "Life has no meaning" or as stirring as Patrick Henry's "Give me liberty or give me death."

Through reading you can transform the darkness of the black ink of the printed word into the light of your mind that illuminates your experience and guides and inspires your thoughts and actions.

Learning to read is like climbing a mountain. From the peak, you can view the accumulated knowledge and wisdom and experiences of all recorded history. You need only open the books, your eyes, your mind, and your heart—and read.

SUGGESTIONS FOR FURTHER STUDY: *Word Power Made Easy* was originally published by Doubleday & Co. If you can't obtain a paperback copy in your local book store, you can order one from:

Mail Service Dept.
Pocket Books, Inc.
1 West 39th Street
New York, New York 10018

Reading to Know and Enjoy

How to Build a Better Vocabulary, by Nurnberg and Rosenblum, was published originally by Prentice Hall, Inc. If you can't obtain a paperback copy locally, you can order one from:

Popular Library, Inc.
355 Lexington Avenue
New York, New York 10017

CHAPTER 5

IN FRANCE, EVEN THE CHILDREN SPEAK FRENCH,
or
How the Experts Learn Languages

A pretty redhead whom I was tutoring told me about a time when she asked her professor for advice on how to study French. Approaching his office, she peeked through the little window in his door. He was only reading a journal; so she knocked timidly.

"Come in," he growled.

Slowly she opened the door and tiptoed into his office.

"What do you want?" he demanded.

"Well, I—uh—, you know I'm not doing very well in French and . . ."

"Yes," he muttered, scarcely raising his eyes from his journal.

"And I just thought you might give me some suggestions about how to study, and uh," she stuttered and paused, embarrassed by her need to ask for help.

The professor looked up at her over his heavy, horn-rimmed glasses. "Miss Adams, have you ever tried," he paused for emphasis and began again; "have you ever tried opening your book?"

In France, Even the Children Speak French

She could feel her face flush with anger and embarrassment. "You know I have," she whispered, retreating through the door.

"Then," he said scornfully, "I would suggest that you try it more often."

Apparently happy with this witticism, he smiled slightly. "Good-bye," he said sarcastically. Having given his advice, he returned to his reading.

The enraged redhead resisted a strong temptation to slam the door as hard as she could.

Fortunately, I'd felt the same kind of frustration that caused her to ask her professor for help. And the way I'd learned to approach language study proved a big help to her. But I must admit that her professor's reaction is not very common.

Most professors are happy to give whatever suggestions they can. In this chapter, though, we're not concerned with what professors can *tell* us. Instead, we're going to be concerned with what the experts can *show* us about learning a language. And who are these experts? The children.

Children, alas, can't tell us how they learn languages so easily. In fact, some people who learn any subject with ease seem to have trouble *telling* us how they learn it, although, sometimes, they may be able to *show* us how they learn. I suspect that learning is largely a private matter, and that you really learn only by being shown or observing on your own—*and by doing*.

Let me show you how I discovered what children do to learn a foreign language. You may be dubious of a normal farm boy who would sit home studying a foreign language by records. So first let me give you a little background about how I came to be doing that.

A couple of days before Christmas, back when I was fourteen, my cousin and I went hunting rabbits with a single-shot twenty-two. But somehow it was I—and not a rabbit—that got shot. The bullet passed so near my spinal cord that I didn't get back to a regular school for more than six years.

One day while waiting for a doctor more than a year later, I ran across a Cortina ad for a commercial Spanish course. One of the farmers in our neighborhood was from Spain, and my high school didn't offer a course in Spanish. So suddenly I began to think I'd like to learn the language.

I wrote to the Cortina Company and found out that they sold the course with a money-back guarantee of satisfaction. And, more important, I could buy it on a monthly payment plan. When I talked it over with my parents, my father was willing for me to take the course—and pay for it with my mother's egg money! My mother finally agreed to the monthly payment idea, too.

When the course came at last, I could hardly wait to unpack the records and books and wind up our old non-electric Victrola.

"Lección primera," the record boomed as loudly as a mechanical phonograph could make it. I grinned happily as it continued with the ABC's in Spanish. Then I listened to a list of words on travel and the family.

My enthusiasm fell off pretty quickly, but I wasn't about to let my parents know. I was soon trying to keep them from seeing me scowling at the book. The first day I spent a couple of hours listening to the voice on the records say slowly and distinctly, *"El hombre, la mujer, el padre, la madre,"* and so on, while I nodded my head and tried to repeat the Spanish words after the record with my eyes on the column reading, "The man, the woman, the father, the mother . . ." *El hombre* simply equalled the m-a-n. Just like a crossword puzzle, I thought, but I didn't like crossword puzzles.

For a week I struggled wearily through the vocabulary and the conversation on the record. Finally I could think the word *brother,* for instance, when the man on the record said *"hermano."* And *"Yo deseo hablar español"* meant "I wish to speak Spanish," and vice versa. But "I" wasn't referring to me; it was just any old "I."

"I might not be learning much Spanish," I thought, "but I'm certainly getting a lot of exercise cranking up that Victrola." I probably could have passed a test on the first lesson with a fair grade. But it just didn't mean anything to me.

Even after I could translate all the words and sentences of the first lesson, I thought about throwing in the towel and admitting I couldn't learn Spanish.

But finally I decided to give myself one more lesson. If I didn't feel better about it then, I'd let my parents pack up the course and ship it back to New York.

If anything, the second lesson seemed harder. Stubbornly, I wound up the Victrola, slipped the needle into the groove, and listened to the voice on the record screech forth *"Lección segunda"* (lesson two, I thought). *"Vocabulario usado en esta lección"* (vocabulary used in this lesson). *"El comedor,"* the voice on the record would say, and I'd look at the English column and say. "The dining room." "Bebo," the voice would say. "I drink," I'd say to myself. The record would drone on through *ensalada* (salad) to *el desierto* (the dessert). Then the record would go "brump, brump," and I'd turn it off.

Then I'd sigh, take a deep breath, and wind up the Victrola again. This time I'd try to repeat the Spanish words after the speaker.

After the record stopped, I'd take another deep breath, wind up the machine, and start a third time. Only this time I'd look at the English words and try to say the Spanish word just before the speaker on the record would say it. Each time I went through this procedure, there'd be fewer Spanish words whose English equivalents I didn't know. But, each time through, I couldn't remember the Spanish word for butter.

I knew most of the words above and below the word for butter. With the record playing and the Spanish column covered up, I'd look at "The soup" and before the voice on the record would say it, I'd say *"La sopa."* I'd look at "The bread" and say *"El pan"* before the voice did. But when I got to "The butter," I'd bite my lip trying to think of the Spanish word. I'd be just about to remember it, when the voice would boom out, *"La mantequilla"*—most irritatingly.

I became so frustrated that if I'd had a teacher—even like the one at the beginning of this chapter—I'd have been mighty tempted to ask him for a way to remember that confounded word. I'd always heard that the darkest part of the night was right before the morning. And I thought it was high time a little light was dawning.

I gritted my teeth and banged my fist against the Victrola. "I am going to remember you, *mantequilla,*" I almost shouted. And suddenly I thought of the position in the refrigerator where we kept the butter. Mentally I opened the door of the refrigerator and in my mind's eye I saw the butter sitting right below the freezing compartment by a jar of milk. Then I said aloud three or four times, *"La mantequilla, la mantequilla, la mantequilla."*

It worked like a charm. The next time through I had no trouble. But something strange was happening. I'd glance at "the eggs," look up or close my eyes, and visualize two or three eggs while I said aloud *"los huevos."* I'd glance at "the bread" and now visualize a platter of biscuits while I said *"el pan."*

"This is great!" I shouted. This was the best I'd felt about Spanish since I'd put the first record on to play.

"What in the world are you talking about?" my mother asked from an adjoining room.

"I think I've got an idea how to learn this Spanish," I replied with enthusiasm, going into the room where the refrigerator was. I explained to my mother what I'd been doing and what I'd just learned to do.

"Now," I said, "when I get to the word *mantequilla,* I think about some butter and not just about the English word "butter."

"Wouldn't everybody go about it that way?" she asked.

I didn't know. Maybe they would, but I hadn't. But it didn't matter, because I'd found the method for myself, even if other people did it automatically.

But I had another idea. I opened the refrigerator and looked at the jar of milk. *"La leche,"* I said aloud, for mother was used to hearing me talking to myself by now. I looked at the eggs. *"Los huevos,"* I said. And when I looked at that nice, yellow butter, right where I'd imagined it, I said, *"La mantequilla!"*

To me, anyway, all this was a revelation. Now I could hardly wait to get to lesson three. But first I reviewed lesson one. *La madre* was no longer just m-o-t-h-e-r. It was also my own mother, busy in the next room setting the table.

The words I couldn't relate immediately to specific people and things, I tried to visualize as I'd first done with butter and *mantequilla. El hermano* was no longer just b-r-o-t-h-e-r. It was also *my* brother, Morris, whom I could see plainly in my mind's eye. For "a Spaniard" I visualized our neighbor Manuel Garcia as I said *"un español."* For "tomorrow," though, I looked at a calendar and, letting my eye rest on the number for the next day, I said aloud, *"mañana."* When I came to "the train," I visualized an old steam locomotive with a dozen cars behind it at the Hammon, Oklahoma, depot, as I said aloud, *"el tren."*

"Gosh, this is fun," I grinned to myself. Spanish words were beginning to *mean* something to me. The sentences had also begun to take on meaning when I stopped merely equating them to so many English words. I could imagine myself actually speaking to someone as I repeated, *"¿Desea usted hablarme en español?"* (Do you want to talk to me in Spanish?)

Soon I discovered another fascinating thing about learning Spanish. As long as I was looking directly at a Spanish word, *camisa,* for example, or its English equivalent "shirt," I couldn't visualize either the equivalent word or the thing itself. It was as if the visual symbol—*camisa*—of the spoken word paralyzed my mind as long as I looked at the printed word. But if I glanced at the word *camisa,* looked away, and said the Spanish word aloud, I could easily visualize a shirt or connect the Spanish word with my own shirt.

It seemed to take both steps—saying the word aloud in Spanish and visualizing or seeing the object at the same time—to make a word really mean something to me. And when I wanted to think of the Spanish word for shirt, I first visualized one, or looked at my own, and I could hear *camisa* in my mind's ear. An able professor later told me what I was really doing when I said a Spanish word aloud and visualized the object represented. I was getting a "fix" on the word; that is, locating myself in relation to the word.

He said the process was similar to the way a navigator used to find the location of his ship with his sextant. First he established the horizon, and then he intersected this with a sighting at the sun or a star. The angle of intersection, plus a look at his navigation tables, told the navigator where he was.

I found I could learn the conjugations of verbs, as well as words representing objects by taking a kind of sound-sight fix on the verb forms. I didn't just say *yo hablo* (I speak), for instance, *tú hablas* (you speak), *él habla* (he speaks), *nosotros hablamos* (we speak), and so on. Rather I would try to make brief, imaginable sentences out of the forms.

I would imagine myself saying to my brother: *yo hablo español* (I speak Spanish); *tú hablas inglés* (you speak English); *nuestra madre habla inglés* (our mother speaks English); *nosotros hablamos inglés* (we speak English); *ustedes* (my brother, mother, and father) *hablan inglés* (you speak English); *ellos—nuestro padre y nuestra madre—hablan inglés* (they—our father and mother—speak English).

So, after my experience with *mantequilla,* I managed to make what I was learning in Spanish mean something to me. By thinking of real people and real things in connection with the words, I was able to fix the words in my mind.

At the time of my experience with butter and *mantequilla,* I wondered how I could have been so stupid. Here it had taken me almost two weeks to learn that I had to avoid merely equating English words to Spanish words and vice versa—almost two weeks to learn that I had to combine sounds of words with actually seeing the objects or visualizing the objects or situations represented. Mother was probably right, I thought; anybody ought to realize what I'd realized. Even a child would probably have done it the right way much sooner.

In France, Even the Children Speak French

Several years later, while I was studying for a master's degree in Spanish, I found out that one child had learned almost immediately what it took me almost two weeks to learn. Because of my enlightening experience with *mantequilla,* I'd never made below an *A* in a language course. But when a Venezuelan student told me about his son's first encounter with English, I blushed to think I'd been so slow.

Angel (pronounced áhn-hell) was the cute little son of a man we'll call Rodolfo Quintana. Angel was only five years old when Rodolfo, an exile from Venezuela, came to the United States to do graduate work in petroleum engineering, after working for two years in Mexico. Rodolfo was so fascinated by Angel's first real introduction to an Oklahoma child that his eyes twinkled and he smiled a number of times while he told me about it.

Almost before the Quintanas had been able to move into their house, a neighbor and his wife from next door had come over and offered to be of any help they could. Oklahoma hospitality, you know. Rodolfo had to do most of the talking for his family. Elena, his wife, had never studied English; and Antonia, her fifteen-year-old sister, had studied only one year of English in school. Bright-eyed, dark-complexioned little Angel knew scarcely a word of English.

As Elena was brewing a pot of Colombian coffee, Rodolfo told his new neighbors that he hoped Angel could attend grade school for a couple of years to get off to a good start in English. And he was really delighted when they said they had a five-year-old son, Johnny, and four other sons, and that they'd be glad for them to play with Angel.

Angel had been unhappy about leaving his playmates in Mexico. So Rodolfo told his son immediately about Johnny (in Spanish, of course). Angel's eyes brightened. He was so eager to meet a new playmate that he could hardly wait for the adults to finish their coffee.

After the coffee and a little conversation about the University of Oklahoma, Rodolfo and Angel walked next door with their neighbors to meet Johnny, who was now in the backyard by himself tossing a rubber ball against the house and trying to catch it.

"Johnny," his father shouted, "come here and meet our new neighbors." Johnny came running, his ball in his hand.

"Mr. Quintana, Angel, I want to introduce my son Johnny to you."

"Hi," Johnny said.

"Mucho gusto de conocerte" (I'm glad to meet you), Angel said, guessing that he was being introduced but looking a little puzzled about the "Hi."

While the parents talked about the university, pretending to ignore the two little boys, Angel started his conquest of English. *"¿No hablas español?"* (Don't you speak Spanish?), he said to Johnny.

Johnny just looked puzzled and shook his head slightly, probably feeling it was safer to disagree than to agree with a question he didn't understand.

But Angel wasn't one to give up easily. *"¿No hablas español?"* he repeated, with a little irritation in his voice.

Johnny kept shaking his head.

Angel looked a little downcast, as if he were thinking (in Spanish, of course), "Well, I guess that's the way it is." Then his black eyes lit up and he pointed to the ball Johnny was holding in his hand.

"¿Cómo se llama?" (What do you call it?), he asked.

Johnny kept shaking his head.

"¿Cómo se llama?" Angel insisted, sounding slightly disgusted that anyone couldn't understand either Spanish or sign talk.

But now Johnny was beginning to get the idea. "Ball," Johnny smiled.

"Pelota," Angel said. Then he tried, "Bahll."

Johnny snickered. "Not bahll, ball."

Angel grinned and pronounced it a little better. By now they were paying no attention to their parents.

Angel's grin widened as if he'd just learned to play a new

58

game. He pointed to Johnny's cocker spaniel. *"¿Cómo se llama?"* he said rapidly.

"Dog," Johnny grinned.

"Dahg," Angel said.

"No, dog," Johnny corrected, shaking his head but smiling.

"Dohg," Angel tried again.

"Dog," Johnny laughed.

"Dog," Angel said, this time almost exactly like Johnny.

Johnny's freckled face fairly beamed, for he had an idea. Dropping his ball, he took Angel by the hand. "Come, I want to take you to meet my brothers."

"Brozer?" Angel asked, looking first at Johnny and then up at his father.

"Quiere presentarte a sus hermanos," (He wants you to meet his brothers), Rodolfo said.

"Bueno, bueno," Angel shouted with delight.

That evening Angel amazed his mother, Elena, and his Aunt Antonia with the dozens of words he had learned. He must have felt a little like Adam when Adam first told Eve the names he'd given to the cattle and to the fowl and to all the beasts of the fields.

"Pelota se llama, ball," Angel had said, *"perro,* dog; *árbol,* tree; *casa,* house; *hermano,* brozer." (He hadn't mastered the *th* sound of brother yet.) *"Mamá, tú eres* mozer" (Mother, you are "mozer"), he'd said with a grin.

"Papá, tú eres fazer," he said, pointing his finger delightedly at Rodolfo.

As Rodolfo told me this three years later, shortly before he left to return to Venezuela (the political climate had changed), he shook his head. "I cahn't understand," he said, "how my son learned English so fast when his mother still can barely carry on a simple conversation without Angel to translate."

"It is amazing," I nodded, remembering that it had taken me nearly two weeks to start making the kind of sound-sight associations Angel had started making in a couple of minutes.

"Within three months," Rodolfo said, grinning, "the

neighbors were saying that Angel spoke English like a little Okie. Elena was already taking him shopping so he could translate for her."

I'd heard from the Quintanas' neighbors how quickly Angel had learned to speak English, and there was no reason at all to doubt what Rodolfo was saying. "How is Antonia coming along with her English?" I asked Rodolfo.

"She has been attending high school here for two years now, but she does not speak and use the language nearly so well as Angel. And his pronunciation is so much better than mine," he continued, "that people can hardly believe that he spoke no English until three years ago."

"I can't detect any Spanish accent at all in his English," I agreed.

"Angel has done very well in school here, too," Rodolfo said. "Why do you think it is that children learn a language so much more easily than adults?" he looked at me and asked.

"I guess it must have something to do with connecting the spoken word with the thing or situation itself, instead of with the written word in your own language," I suggested, recalling my own experience with *mantequilla.*

But I suppose I never really thought much about the problem other people have in learning a language until I started tutoring Spanish and French about a year later. After *mantequilla,* Spanish had never seemed hard. I'd finished my high-school courses, including two years of French, by correspondence study through the University of Oklahoma Extension Division. I'd gained credit for two years of high-school Spanish by an attainment examination. And I'd enjoyed taking a number of French, Spanish, and Latin courses in the University, but I'd never felt I'd spent too much time with them. In fact, if anything, I'd spent proportionately more time on my other courses.

After tutoring just a few students I began to feel that perhaps my mother was wrong about the way most people approach a foreign language. Maybe they didn't all have the same kind of revelation I'd had with *mantequilla.* Maybe if they didn't know how to read, they'd have to approach a new language as Angel had—or not learn it at all.

After *mantequilla,* studying languages had never seemed like drudgery to me. Could it be, I began to wonder, that many students never get beyond my *mantequilla* stage? Could it be that they keep studying Spanish, or French, or German, as I had studied Spanish my first ten days, before *mantequilla?* Could it be that after weeks or months of studying French, for instance, they were still relating *mère* only to m-o-t-h-e-r?

I was soon to begin getting answers to these questions. "Have you ever related the French word *mère* to your own mother?" I started asking all my French students. "Have you ever related the Spanish word *madre* to your own mother?" I have kept asking all my Spanish students.

All my language students look a little amazed at the question. "No, I've never thought about doing that," about half of them say, shaking their heads. And most of the other half, who *have* made the association, have done so only fleetingly.

The problem is that they've never made a foreign language mean anything to them personally. They've never learned that to make a word or sentence mean something to them they must have more than one image or sense impression of it.

The sound-sight method I've been talking about is almost precisely the way *you* learned English! Now you can no longer recall learning your first words. But probably you can check what I'm about to say by watching some baby learning its first words.

The first two words you learned were probably "mamma" and "daddy." Your mother, no doubt, whispered "mamma, mamma" to you hundreds of times before you began to make some association with the sound "mamma" and the person standing above your crib saying the word to you.

Finally, one happy day for her, you looked up and said "mamma" back to her. You weren't thinking *your* name was "mamma." But somehow, perhaps because she smiled her approval, you realized that "mamma" was the name for that person who spoke the word to you.

At first you may have gotten the idea that "daddy" was another name for your mother. She probably repeated the word "daddy" more times to you than your father did. But soon you sensed your parents' disapproval when you looked up at your mother and said "daddy" or when you looked at your father and said "mamma."

Slowly you realized that to make a word mean something to you, you had to both sound it and experience it by sight or one of the other senses. You learned the meaning of the word "glass" by saying the word and seeing a glass and perhaps feeling it in your hand.

When you started to learn to read, you learned that a word like c-a-t was a visual symbol of the sound "cat," which you already used in talking and thinking about the animal. Perhaps you have now reached the point where the written word c-a-t is a direct symbol of the animal itself. Almost immediately after you see the written word you may visualize the animal.

Why don't most students do the same thing with words in a foreign language? From questioning them and remembering what I did before *mantequilla,* the best explanation I can figure out is this. The student sees the word *gato,* for instance, and looks away. Then what he sees in his mind's eye is not the animal but the English word "cat." The mind has taken the same number of steps; there's a translation, but *no meaning.*

Where there's no meaning, of course, you have as much trouble remembering something as you would remembering a list of names picked at random from a telephone directory. To make new foreign words and sentences mean something to you, try these four simple rules:

1) Glance at the word or sentence in your book.
2) Look away from your book or close your eyes.
3) Say the word or sentence aloud as you visualize the object or situation represented. Remember, the more

personal and specific you can make it, the better.

4) When you are not studying, practice saying aloud the foreign words and expressions that fit the objects or situations you are looking at.

Childish? No. Childlike? Maybe so. But my students and I have found it the best way of imitating the real experts at language learning—the children.

This approach is not the only suggestion I have about studying a foreign language. (I'll give you several others in the next chapter.) But all the others together are not nearly as important as those we've discussed in this chapter.

I hope your reaction to all this is much like that of a pre-medical student I tutored. At the end of our first session, after I'd gone over most of the points covered here, he was nodding his head seriously.

"I think maybe you're right," he said, smiling. "I've heard that in France, even the children speak French." He leaned back, took a deep breath, and continued. "If I tried, surely I could learn as well as a child."

Then he paused and rubbed his forehead thoughtfully. "Maybe what that professor said about your other student applies to me. I suppose I do need to open my book more often," he continued. "But I guess I'll just have to go back to my room and try doing it *your* way."

"The children's way," I corrected.

"I'd sure like to learn Spanish well enough to pull an *A*," he said hopefully.

And he did.

SUGGESTION: Readers interested in more information about Cortina language courses may write to R.D. Cortina Academy of Languages, 136 52nd Street, New York, N.Y. 10019.

CHAPTER 6

MORE WAYS TO IMPROVE
YOUR LANGUAGE-LEARNING ABILITY

"What *is* language-learning ability?" I have often asked myself. In fact, I started toying with that question right after I began tutoring several years ago. I didn't think that language-learning ability necessarily has anything to do with a student's age when he first starts to learn a second language.

But after I had tutored my first few dozen students in Spanish and French, I was beginning to get the idea that the older a person is when he starts studying his first foreign language the more difficult it is for him.

One October evening, though, this idea was knocked right out of the window. It happened this way.

Lee, one of my math students, had cleared up all the calculus problems that were bothering him, and he and I were chatting while I waited for my next student.

"How is your German coming along?" I asked, remembering that he was taking German and thinking that I might give him a useful suggestion or two.

"You know," he said, lighting a cigarette, "I think I have an *A* going in that class."

"Really?" I said, probably letting a little surprise show in my voice. Lee was twenty-five and had worked on his father's wheat and dairy farm for six years after high school and marriage before he decided to go to college. He was doing no better than a *B*- in math, which he was planning to teach in high school. So I was a little astonished about his German grade.

"Yes, I was a little surprised myself when I got *A's* on my last two tests," he admitted.

"That's really good," I said, hoping my voice didn't reveal any lingering doubts about his report. "You must be studying the right way. Just how are you going about it?"

He leaned back in his chair, exhaling a smoke ring. "The funny thing is that I don't spend as much time actually studying German as I spend with math. Working fifteen hours a week, I don't have as much time for study as I'd like to have."

"I knew you were working in a garage," I said, nodding.

"But I manage to think about my German quite a bit when I'm not actually studying it," he went on.

"Oh? How do you manage that?" I asked, wondering if perhaps he did have a secret or two that I might file away in my mind to disclose later to other language students.

He frowned a moment. "I wouldn't tell just anyone, because they might think it was silly. But since you're interested in the way people learn, maybe it won't seem silly to you."

"No, I am sure it wouldn't at all!" I exclaimed. "When it comes to learning, I guess I'm what they call a pragmatist. Any way that works well for a student is a good way, in my books."

"Well," he said slowly, "at times I try to pretend I'm a German, and I give names in German to things I can see, especially when I'm going to German class. You might say I try to see in German."

"See in German?" I caught my breath. "Could you give me some examples?"

"Well, when I'm walking across the campus from the parking lot to Kaufman Hall, for example, I try to say to myself the German words for tree and sky and building and grass and girl—whatever I happen to see."

"I think that's an excellent idea," I interrupted, catching on quickly.

"Oh yes," he went on, "and while I'm waiting for class to start, I try to translate snatches of conversation I overhear into German." He grinned at that, obviously with some amusing, private memories.

"You're going against a theory of mine," I exclaimed.

"You mean there's something wrong with doing this, you think?" Lee frowned.

"Not in the least!" I shook my head. "You're doing *exactly* the sort of thing I try to get my French and Spanish students to do," I said and laughed. "Did anyone give you the idea?"

"No," he paused, "I don't think so. If someone had, I probably wouldn't have thought what I was doing was silly. But I knew it seemed to help me."

"It isn't silly; it's smart," I insisted. "After all, why study a language if you don't at least entertain the possibility of putting it to use?"

"I guess a lot of students study a foreign language only because they have to, but I made up my mind to learn German the best I could. You don't start to college at twenty-four unless you've made up your mind you want to learn."

"Well, you're off to a good start," I complimented him, no longer having the slightest doubt about his *A* in the course. "But as I started to say, you *are* going against a theory I was beginning to hold."

"What theory was that?" he asked, wrinkling his forehead.

"I believed the older a student is when he starts studying his first foreign language, the more likely his approach is to be bad. But you're using your imagination in an effective sort of way that a lot of students who started their first foreign language in junior high never think of doing."

"I'm glad to know that, and I'll be sure to try to keep it up," he said thoughtfully. "But maybe you have some ideas on studying the text that I might find helpful."

Before I had a chance to make any suggestions, my next student arrived. So I had to wait until my next appointment with Lee to give him the suggestions I'm going to give you about using textbooks.

Many language textbooks for beginners start each lesson with a half page or so of reading material in the language. Then there is a list of new vocabulary words, followed by an explanation of new points of grammar. Next come questions in the foreign language on the reading material, and then various exercises involving conjugations, fill-ins, and so forth. Finally several sentences are given to be translated from English into the foreign language. Usually this last exercise is the one required to be written out and handed in or discussed in class.

Assuming that the authors of the textbook have some reason for putting the reading exercise first, students usually take a quick glance at it, decide it's too difficult to grasp without further help, and hasten on to the vocabulary list, trying to memorize the new words with no other association than with English *words.* The next thing they tend to do is to read quickly the grammatical explanations and then to start on the translation of the English sentences into the foreign language. Dutiful, they want to make sure they finish the assignment, whether they learn much or not.

Little wonder that many such students decide that learning a foreign language is almost impossibly difficult! They have reversed the approach intended by the authors of the text. They shouldn't have to be told, but they need to be: The effective way to study a language lesson is to start at the beginning and to work *forward.* Learn in the same direction as a child learns. That's the key.

Suppose your beginning language text is not arranged like the type just discussed. If it is one with a beginning dialogue translated into English, you may find it best to read the English translation three or four times, visualizing the scene and participants as vividly as possible. Then when you can repeat the translation in English almost word for word while visualizing the scene, read the foreign-language section, relating the words not just to the English words but to your mental pictures suggested by the English dialogue. Repeat the dialogue in the foreign language until you can recite it almost word for word while seeing and hearing in your mind the participants in the dialogue.

When you begin a study period on a foreign language, it is best not to begin with a new lesson. Instead, start a couple of lessons back (in lesson three if you are assigned lesson five), and then work forward. Thus you warm yourself up to the language by a quick rereading of the foreign language reading material at the beginning of lessons three and four. Now you're ready to begin the first part of lesson five.

"Why worry about the reading in the foreign language before you know the new vocabulary?" you may be inclined to ask.

Let me answer that with questions to you: "How have you learned most of the words you know in English? Have you learned them by looking them up in a dictionary?"

Of course not. Most of the words you know—probably more than 90 percent of them—you learned from context. That is, when you ran across a new word, you had a pretty good idea of its meaning from the meanings of the words around it, from the way it was used in the sentence. The more times you noticed its being used, the more certain you became of its meaning. Finally you became so certain of it, if it is in your active vocabulary, that you dared to use it in writing or conversation.

"I've looked up a lot of words!" you may protest.

"Yes, but where did you find them to look up—in a word list?" I ask.

Almost certainly not. Most of the words that you've learned

by looking them up in a dictionary you found *first* in sentences. And if you are like me, sometimes you may have had to look up words used in the definition, and in that way you learned more words than you intended. This is why I insist on the importance of reading the foreign-language material at the beginning of a lesson before studying the vocabulary.

Summarizing, then, for most foreign-language textbooks, this is the way I suggest that you proceed. First, read through the foreign-language section without worrying about any of the words you don't know. You should be trying only to get an idea about what is being discussed.

Next, start at the beginning of the material and read through an entire sentence. If you find one or more new words, *first try to make a good guess at their meanings.* Only now should you try to find the word in the vocabulary list that follows the reading material. Don't worry if your guess is wrong. It is the fact that you have guessed in terms of the surrounding words that helps fix the right meaning in your mind.

After you have found the new words, read the entire sentence aloud. Then go on to the next sentence and proceed as before.

When you have finished the last sentence, start on the reading material for a third time. This time you'll probably be able to read through the material with a complete understanding. As you read, try to see in your mind's eye and hear in your mind's ear whatever is being described or discussed in the foreign language.

If your school has a language laboratory or if you can obtain records or tapes that go with your text, by all means try to use them. I started both Spanish and French with records; so I discovered early that listening to a sentence while you picture what is going on is a great help in fixing the words and patterns of the language in your mind.

After you've carefully studied the opening section of your lesson, go next to the vocabulary list for that lesson. I suggest that you take a sheet of paper or a small card and cover up the English words. If you're studying Spanish, for example, and you have "the letter" on the English side of the vocabulary list, picture in your mind a letter addressed to you. Then try to recall the sentence in the lesson in which the word was used. Now say *la carta* while you keep in your mind a mental picture of a letter.

If you fail to recall a word in the foreign language, try to glance quickly over the reading material until you discover it. Only as a last resort (or to check a good guess) should you look at the foreign word that you are trying to recall.

If you have trouble recalling a foreign word from its English equivalent, put a pencil dot by the English word, and start a record of troublesome words. Later, in reviewing, if you should have trouble with the same word again, put another pencil dot by it. Thus you can soon spot at a glance the words that trouble you most.

After a list of new words most language texts for beginners go into an explanation of new points of grammar. Occasionally, but not often, you may have to read the explanation *before* you can understand the reading material at the beginning of the lesson. More important than the rules of grammar are the brief examples that illustrate the rules, for, as in English grammar, we can often recall an example more easily than a rule.

Suppose you have the Spanish rule about using a form of *estar* (to be) in expressing location, and the example is *La carta está sobre la mesa.* Imagine a letter lying on your table, and say the Spanish sentence to yourself until you can recall the mental picture when you see the Spanish sentence. Later when you need to apply the rule, you'll probably recall the example and then the rule. If you memorize a rule without an example to go with it, often you will fail to realize you need to apply the rule. So when you learn a rule, be sure to memorize the example that goes with it; then try to compose a similar example from your own experience. For example, *Mi primo Roberto está en*

Chicago (My cousin Robert is in Chicago).

In reviewing rules of grammar, the most effective method is to look at the English translation of the example sentence (with the example itself covered up) and try to recall the foreign-language example. If you make a mistake, put a pencil dot at the beginning or end of the English phrase or sentence so that you will have a record of your trouble spots.

Most textbooks have questions in the foreign language immediately before or after the grammar section. The questions are probably the most neglected part of a lesson. Here is a chance to keep all your thinking in the foreign language. Usually the answer to a question involves simply a rearrangement of a few words of the question plus another word or two from the reading material. *"¿Dónde están Roberto y Luis?"* (Where are Robert and Louis?) an exercise may ask. Preferably without translating, you begin your answer, *"Roberto y Luis están . . ."* (Robert and Louis are . . .), and by now you've probably recalled that *dónde* means "where" and that in the reading material Robert and Louis are in the park. If you're doing the exercise in the most effective way possible, you *see* them in the park (in your mind's eye), perhaps under a tall tree standing by a park bench, and now you can finish your sentence: *"Roberto y Luis están en el parque."*

You may find it well worth your while to write out your answers to the questions in a notebook, for many teachers ask the same or similar questions on dictated parts of a quiz. Often students do poorly on this part of the quiz because they attempt to translate the question into English before answering it in the foreign language. The trouble is that they are often still trying to translate the last question when the teacher goes on to the next one.

This problem has a simple solution. When the teacher first asks the question, listen only for the subject of the question and the verb, and repeat them quickly to yourself. If the question is directed to you, of course, begin your answer with the appropriate form of the translation of "I" or "we" and the

71

correct verb form. Your teacher may ask, for example, *"¿A qué hora va usted a la clase?"* (What time do you go to class?) As soon as you hear *usted,* you know your reply will begin with *yo* (I), or, since this is Spanish, you may leave off the pronoun; but you have to have the verb form of *ir* (to go) that is used with *yo.* So before the teacher starts to repeat the question, you have the beginning of your answer: *Yo voy a la clase* .... When your teacher repeats the question, you concentrate on the first part: *"¿A qué hora...."* Realizing that it is asking "when" if you didn't get it the first time, you can give your answer any appropriate hour: *"Yo voy a la clase a las ocho."* (I am going to class at eight o'clock.)

If the question is about something or some third person or persons, use the same subject or an appropriate subject pronoun to start your answer, and the verb form remains the same. Suppose your teacher asks, *"¿Dónde viven los padres de María?"* Mentally you grab onto the phrase *los padres de María* without worrying about translation. If you have time, you write, *"Los padres de María...."* Before the teacher can repeat the question, you have probably guessed or recalled that it begins with *dónde.* Having done the exercises carefully, you can recall the phrase that completes the answer. And triumphantly you can write, *"Los padres de María viven cerca del parque."* (Mary's parents live near the park.)

If the question does not begin with an interrogative such as "who," "what," "when," or "where," you will probably have even less trouble. If your teacher asks, for example, *"¿Es señor usted mejicano?"* you need only to change the pronoun and verb and make your answer negative: *"No, señor, no soy mejicano."* (No, sir, I am not a Mexican.)

Don't neglect any of the exercises just because you think they are repetitious. Of course they are repetitious. They are meant to be! It is only through repetition that you can fix the patterns of a language in your mind.

You can fix wrong patterns in your mind as well as correct patterns. That is why you should keep a notebook with corrections to exercises. In first doing an exercise, write on every other line or every third line, leaving the lines in between for your corrections. In reviewing, study the corrected copy to learn the pattern, paying a little attention to the mistakes you made earlier so that you can avoid them next time.

To fix correct patterns in your mind, you should often review the reading material at the beginning of the lessons. There is no substitute for repetition in learning a language. It is through repeatedly seeing and hearing and using a word that you learn a word in English. And it is through repeatedly seeing and hearing and using words that you learn them in a foreign language. So don't think the authors of your text stupid for including so many little exercises. They are for *your* benefit!

And remember too that it is the first time through an exercise that requires the most effort and produces the least return. The second time through you spend much less effort and accomplish much more. *It is repetition that fixes the words and patterns in your mind.* Perhaps that is why one of the most famous lines from modern literature is Gertrude Stein's "A rose is a rose is a rose."

In many language texts the last exercise of a lesson consists of translating English into the foreign language. If you have done the other exercises thoroughly, this translation should go pretty quickly. But remember to do the translation in your notebook on every other line so that you will have plenty of room for corrections.

"How in the world am I going to find time to study lessons like this?" you may be asking with discouragement.

Take it from me that the methods I've pointed out save time and prevent frustration in the long run. They save you from starting backwards and from the annoyance of turning pages repeatedly to look up words and rules and examples that fail to stick in your mind even after you've looked them up.

The wrong way is the backward way. The right way is the forward way. The right way is to start at the beginning of the lesson, as the author intended, and to work carefully and imaginatively through the exercises.

This was the way—I found out the next time I saw my twenty-five-year-old math student—that Lee was approaching the lessons in his German textbook, and it was the way I had studied my language lessons.

I wasn't able to give Lee many suggestions to improve his study of German, because, fortunately, he had started with good methods. He did think it was a good idea not only to see and hear in German, but to feel, taste, and smell in German as well! Although I was unable to help Lee improve on his methods, he helped me to help other students and, I hope, to help you.

Lee made me realize better than anyone else that the important characteristics of a good language student are enthusiasm, imagination, foresightedness in organization of study time, and willingness to *use* the language.

All of this suggests that you don't have to be unusually smart to be an excellent language student. Some of the Spanish and French majors I have known made excellent grades in languages; but with as much or more effort, they made only average grades in history or the sciences, for example. I know one boy who made a *B* in beginning Spanish while flunking freshman English!

On the other hand, I have tutored many science and pre-med majors who were having far more difficulty with Spanish or French than they should have had. One pretty blonde majoring in math couldn't understand why she was making a *C* in French, while with the same amount of effort she was making an *A* in math. When at my suggestion she started making the language personal rather than impersonal and objective like a science, she soon understood why she had been having so much trouble.

Invariably such students as she had been attempting to learn the language by memorizing (not associating) vocabulary and rules of verb conjugations, and had been trying to juggle words until everything was right. Maybe a language can be learned by that kind of crossword-puzzle approach, but it cannot be learned efficiently.

At the risk of repeating myself from the last chapter, I say again: You have to make a language mean something to you *personally,* and you have to get a little emotion and feeling attached to the words and ideas if you want to learn a language with the greatest amount of ease and satisfaction. Just as Lee learned to see in German, you learn to perceive in the language you're studying. Take *naranja* (Spanish for "orange"), for example. In your imagination you see it, feel it, taste it, and smell it. And when you get a chance, not only do you imagine *una naranja* but you apply the word to a real *naranja!*

Let me mention a few things now that will help you when you start using the separate readers that go with some courses. If you have four or five pages assigned in a Spanish reader, for example, first read all the assignment without looking up any words. Read just to get an idea of what is going on. The next time through, read more carefully sentence by sentence, making sure to guess at any words you don't know before you look them up. *And do avoid writing the English translation of words between the lines.* If you must write the translations on the same page, number the words bothering you and write their translations in the margins.

But much better still, keep a notebook with the name of the story at the top of the page and the page number in your reader where the new words are found. Write the foreign words on the left-hand side, leaving a generous amount of space before you write the English translation. Here's how your page would look:

El Camino

p. 14	a menudo	often
	un cocido	stew, a good meal
	un quesero	a cheese maker
	un herrero	a blacksmith
	se embustiese (from embustirse)	might deceive himself (to deceive oneself)

remendado	mended
desempeñar	to carry out
enamoriscado	slightly in love
rostritorcido	crooked faced
le dio calabazas (from darle calabazas a)	jilted him (from, literally, to give him pumpkins— to jilt)

Thus you can cover up with a card either the foreign words or the English words and find how many words you can recall when you review. In the process of reviewing, you can put a pencil dot by the words you have trouble translating, just as you do with the vocabulary lists in the lessons of your textbook.

So you read through the assignment sentence by sentence, looking up at least those new words that seem essential to an understanding of the sentence and making good guesses at the meanings of all the new words. Then you read the assignment a third time with complete or almost complete understanding. As in the regular lesson material, the more repetition you undergo the better you fix the words and patterns of the language in your mind. And that's what you are trying to do.

After two semesters of college work in a foreign language or two years of high-school work, you will find it useful and stimulating to use a dictionary in the language you are studying; that is, one that defines the words in the same language, as an English dictionary defines words in English. Just as in English, when you look up a word or phrase in such a dictionary, you find new ways of expressing an idea in the foreign language.

For example, if you look up the Spanish word *menudo* in an all-Spanish dictionary, you find under the phrase *a menudo* the definition *con frecuencia.* Knowing that *con* means "with," you don't have to use much imagination to realize that *frecuencia* means "frequency."

More Ways to Improve Your Language-Learning Ability

You may find yourself looking up words used in a definition, but I can think of few more fascinating and effective ways of adding to your command of the language. If you can avoid the translation habit, using a dictionary all in the foreign language gives you a good opportunity to think in the language.

As you move into a third or fourth semester of a foreign language, you will be surprised how much you can understand in a newspaper or magazine in the language even without looking up words. And if your school has stressed understanding of the spoken language, or if you have used records of your own, you will be surprised also by how much you can grasp of radio programs or movies in the language. Not only will you be pleased by how much you can understand, you will be even more pleased by how much your understanding improves after only a few hours of reading newspapers, magazines, or books in the language, even if you only guess at the unfamiliar words from context and do not look them up.

Let me give you some personal examples. When I started college, I had credit for two years of Spanish and two years of French, both of which I studied by myself with the aid of textbooks, records, and radio. So in my freshman year of college I took two reading courses in both languages. In my sophomore year I did not take any courses in Spanish or French, but I did most of my outside reading for two survey courses in European history in Spanish and French. Though I looked up very few words as I read history books in Spanish and French, I feel I added more to my vocabulary and knowledge of the languages than I had in the reading courses for which I received college credit in the languages.

Soon I was enjoying conversing in Spanish with Latin American students and in French with students at the French club. Many high schools and universities have language clubs that give students a chance to express themselves in a foreign language and to listen to it without worrying about being graded on their efforts.

77

Language study, then, is intended to give you command of the language for your *personal* use in reading, experiencing, and expressing yourself. When you start dreaming in a foreign language, you are really making progress!

Right now, though, efficient *personal* use of a foreign language may be only a daydream for you, but you can make it into a reality. Here, in summary, are steps to follow in studying the regular textbook to help make a reality of that daydream:

1) Warm up by rereading the foreign-language material in the two or three previous lessons;
2) Read the foreign-language material at the beginning of the lesson once for a general idea of what it's about;
3) Read the same material a second time sentence by sentence, guessing at any new words before you check your guess against the vocabulary list, the English translation, the glossary in the back of the book, or a dictionary;
4) Read the material a third or fourth time, perhaps aloud, with complete understanding;
5) Do the repetitious exercises with a willing heart;
6) Write your exercises in a notebook on every second or third line so that you can make corrections neatly and can learn from your mistakes.

In using the foreign-language reader, apply as many of the steps above as you can.

With a conscientious trial of the methods, I feel sure that you'll agree with a little formula of mine that answers the question, "What is language-learning ability?" The formula is simple to remember, for it consists of the English vowels:

$$a=e+i+o+u,$$

where *a* stands for ability, *e* for enthusiasm, *i* for imagination, *o* for organization, and *u* for use. That is, ability is influenced by your enthusiasm, your imagination, your organization, and your use of the language. (This is true not only of language, as you'll see in chapters to come.)

In these two chapters on language study, you've been learning how to improve all these elements, which really reinforce each other. Now it's up to you.

CHAPTER 7

MATHEMATICS AND THE THINGS YOU LEARN

Do you ever need directions to get to some place? If so, you are concerned with location, and location is concerned with math.

Do you ever use a watch or calendar? If so, you are concerned about where you are in time, and location in time is a matter of mathematics.

Do you keep a record on the stubs of the checks you write? If you do, then in your efforts to find where you are financially you use some wonderful tools of math unknown in England before 1400.

Have you ever been curious about the statement that the modern electronic digital computer is based on a system of counting that's simpler than our system of tens, hundreds, and thousands? If so, you've been curious about a very important but simple principle of mathematics.

When you think about how much your life and your learning are related to mathematics, you are not very surprised to learn that the word "mathematics" comes from an old Greek word *mathematikos,* meaning "disposed or inclined to learn." (You are, or you wouldn't be reading this!) *Mathematikos* itself comes from *mathemata,* meaning things learned, and certainly you want to add to *your* things learned. Finally, "mathematics" can be traced back to the Greek word *manthanein,* meaning "to learn."

Nearly all your learning is concerned with locating yourself in relation to places, people, languages, and ideas. When you are traveling, you refer to maps to find where you are. You like to know what people think of you so that you can know *where you stand* in their affections. If you learn a language in a foreign country, you learn it so you can *find* yourself in relation to things and people in terms of the local language. If you study philosophy, history, or religion, for instance, because you really want to, you study so that you will feel comfortable and at home with ideas you've been curious about.

Often a person has to locate himself better in regard to math before he can make much more use of it in relation to his other learning. Yes, it is a required subject for many of us. But even if it were not and if you could locate yourself well in terms of the math you've already been exposed to, I think you'd really want to know more about math than you do.

You may be required to pass a certain number of math courses. So, at least, you have some idea of where you want to go mathematically. I've always heard that it is much easier to get where you want to go when you know where you are to start with.

Above all else, then, the math chapters in this book are intended to help you find where you are mathematically and, in addition, to give you some signposts to guide you along the way.

You've probably heard stories of the hillbilly who is so ignorant that he doesn't know his left hand from his right hand. In fact, it's probably more important to him to know which ways are east, west, north, and south than to know left from right. If he didn't know his directions, his neighbors would think he was really ignorant!

As you may know, rural and small-town people believe that it is as important to know where you are, to know what direction places are relative to you, as it is to know your left side from your right side. In the country, you are lost if you don't know your directions.

So the rural people watching "Candid Camera," a popular TV program at one time, were highly amused one night when a man asked New Yorkers on the street about the directions. They could all distinguish east and west, but twenty-five out of twenty-six New Yorkers interviewed had pointed across the street to the south and called it north!

If you rarely get to see the North Star or the Big Dipper, and if you can't remember whether the shadow of the sun is to the north or to the south, I have a simple way for you to determine directions. The sun, of course, comes up in either the east, the northeast, or the southeast regardless of where you are in the world. If you know that you are on an east-west street, for example, face the approximate direction the sun rises from and raise your arms. Now your left arm points north and your right arm points south. This method is much more sporting than using a compass.

This book is concerned primarily with making you aware of your need to use your senses and sense images (come to think of it, there isn't any other kind) and your need for considering things from different angles in locating yourself; that is, in learning.

To locate yourself accurately, you must use at least two senses. Usually one is seeing and the other is hearing. As you've learned in the first chapter on language study, a word is a kind of intersection between sight and sound. You can see well only a small area in the direct line of your vision, but you can hear from all directions. So hearing is at least as important as seeing to the kind of locating we call learning. Understanding is always strongly reinforced when we write things down in our own words, or make sketches, or when we say things aloud.

Painting, for instance, is visual, but you add to your enjoyment of it when you *talk* about it and make an effort to describe it in words. Music has to do with sound, but the musical score is visual, and a performance you see is somehow more moving than one you only hear. All experience is enriched if you bring to bear both your sense of seeing and your sense of hearing.

If you can locate yourself by sight, good. If you can locate yourself by sound, fine. But remember that *you locate yourself best by using all your senses.* And memory itself is best served by bringing to bear as many senses as you can.

Have you ever noticed, for example, how people remember telephone numbers? Trying to recall an unfamiliar number, some people close their eyes and visualize the number as if they were projecting it on the back of their eyelids. Others say the number aloud or to themselves, remembering it by the way it sounds. Still others remember the number by how far their dialing finger moves on the dial, a kind of muscle memory involving feeling.

But the people who remember telephone numbers and other things best combine *sight, sound, feeling,* and occasionally *taste,* and *smell.* If they fail to remember something because one sense impression fails them, they still have at least one or two others to try.

Likewise, to learn math effectively you have to make use of more than one sense. You can build knowledge effectively only on what is familiar and comfortable.

Math involves a number of abstractions, and sometimes abstractions of abstractions. Let me show you what I mean. First we learn, or we should learn, to count in relation to objects. Counting deals with objective numbers. In algebra we have letter values—such as *a, b, x,* and *y*—representing throughout a problem specific numbers unknown at the beginning of the problem. Algebra deals with subjective numbers. Later we have problems whose letter values may depend on another letter value that can represent an infinite number of numerical values in a problem.

It may sound complicated, but if you build your foundations solidly and keep them in good repair, you can keep adding safely to the structure of your mathematical knowledge. With effort the foundations themsleves can be bolstered and strengthened.

It is amazing how people with just average intelligence can build in their own minds structures of mathematical knowledge that required man thousands of years to come by. The reason that a person can build such a structure is that the blueprints are already drawn for him, but the foundations must be laid in his senses and experiences and the new parts firmly put into place.

Important to the building of your own mathematical structure are the wonderful mathematical tools at your disposal. In the third grade you were already using confidently tools of mathematics that were unknown to the Greeks and even to the British until about the 1490's-the Gobar numerals (or so-called Arabic numerals).

Where you build your mathematical knowledge with comparative ease, men put forth great effort just chiseling out the tools. You should realize that you don't have to be some sort of genius to follow the blueprints of much of the mathematical structure that is your heritage once you learn to use the tools and understand the language of mathematics.

It is important also for you to realize that you are wrong if you have the impression from some math textbooks that the rules of mathematics were handed to a few geniuses by the gods, as the Ten Commandments were given to Moses. It just isn't so.

The beginnings of math, you might be surprised to know, date back to long before the existence of man on Earth. In fact, some animals *inherit* their mathematical knowledge. (No doubt you'd like that!) For example, honey bees locate themselves instinctively by the angle of the sun's rays, their compound eyes serving as a kind of sextant. They have a built-in sense of time that enables them to make adjustments for changes in the sun's position during long flights. And they tell their hive mates by a dance the direction and approximate distance of a supply of nectar and how good it is. The other worker bees know instinctively how to interpret the dances.

Scientists have found that some migratory birds locate themselves by the position of the stars; that is, by vision. They inherit knowledge, if it can be called that, of how to orient themselves in relation to a pattern of stars. Thus they can fly from their summer homes where they are hatched to their winter home.

Exactly how some birds, such as the homing pigeon, and homing cats and dogs locate themselves is not known. But they do locate themselves and find their way. And we know that bats use sound, much as planes use radar, to locate themselves.

But the only way birds have of communicating their knowledge or awareness of where they are and where they should go is by taking off and flying some place. If other birds learn from them, they learn by following. Fish, dogs, perhaps most animals, have means of finding their way that man can only guess at.

Man, though, was the first creature to be able to show his fellow beings *how* he found his way by landmarks, by sun, and by stars. Like the animals, his first use of what we call math was to locate himself.

You see, man had little need to count beyond the sum of his fingers or toes until he became a herder of sheep. To count he had to invent names, that is make sounds for different numbers of animals. Numbers like one, two, and three were a kind of intersection between the sounds man made and nearby objects like stones or sheep.

When some men turned from nomadic sheep herding to growing crops of corn or wheat, they needed to be able to predict the seasons in order to know when to sow. And the Egyptians found that they needed also to find whose land was whose after each of the Nile floods. In short, they found it necessary to turn their attention from the objective numbers of counting to subjective numbers of measurement. Thus they developed many of the principles of plane geometry, or earth measurement (from the Greek words *ge,* meaning the earth, plus *metrein,* to measure); but they didn't write much of it down, leaving some huge piles of stones, called pyramids, to show us that they knew plenty about astronomy and geometry.

The Greeks took Egyptian geometry, objectified it into lines and points on paper, formalized and systematized it, added to it, and almost tried to make a religion out of it. From the personal gods like Zeus, Athena, and Apollo, the Greeks turned to abstract numbers and lines about the time of Pythagoras. From Pythagoras, of the Pythagorean theorem (569-500 B.C.), to Euclid (c. 330-275 B.C.), the Greeks made geometry a kind of Goddess of Reason.

Not long afterwards, though, at the University of Alexandria, in Egypt, some Greeks brought measurement back to math and math back to astronomy. Trigonometry (three-angle measurement) was the result—this, mind you, before the birth of Christ! Why, Erastothenes (275-194 B.C.) got a measure of the circumference of the earth that was only about fifty miles off the value accepted today—seventeen-hundred years before Columbus' famous voyage.

The ancient Greeks and Egyptians were so busy looking at the stars and drawing lines in the sand that they didn't do much about their horrible system of writing numbers. They still added and subtracted on an abacus, forms of which primitive peoples used before the dawn of recorded history. (The modern abacus, still used widely in the Orient, consists of counting beads on strings stretched between wooden or plastic frames.) Today, you don't even see Roman numerals much—except on old ' movies, where they don't want you to know how old!—and Greek numerals you see not at all.

A hundred or so years after Erastothenes, some lazy, practical Hindu got tired of carrying an abacus around to count, turned his attention from the stars, and made one of the most important discoveries in math, a symbol for the empty column on the abacus. We call it zero today. Out of this discovery the Hindus developed the positional counting you learned in grade school and freed themselves from dependence on an abacus for their calculations.

Imagine trying to do arithmetic with Roman numerals. In fact, arithmetic as you learned it in grade school didn't exist at the time of the Romans. Arithmetic had to wait another fifteen hundred years!

The Arabs learned the geometry of the Greeks and the Hindu way of writing numbers. Later, forbidden by the teachings of Mohammed to make pictures of living things, the Arabs emphasized the aural and near aspects of math and developed a branch of math that has no lines. They called it algebra just as we do today. The Arabs produced great astronomers and physicians as well as mathematicians. Their universities in Spain became so famous that Catholic monks disguised themselves as Mohammedans to attend the Moorish universities and find out about this learning.

So knowledge or trigonometry, algebra, and astronomy reached the mathematically backward Europeans. The Europeans, though, introduced the "+" and "−" signs about the time of Columbus' voyage and the "x" and "=" signs about a hundred years later. Finally, man had the symbols you learned in grade-school arithmetic!

But these new symbols were not really popularized until after much study the Frenchman René Descartes (1596-1650) conceived in three dreams the brilliant idea of combining geometry and algebra (the visual and the aural) into a new math he called analytic geometry (published in 1637). Unlike Euclid, whom the math textbook writers have followed for centuries, Descartes disclosed his methods of reasoning.

About a hundred and twenty-five years later, Newton applied Descartes' math to problems in astronomy, learning why the apple falls, and found that he needed to go a step further. The result was the calculus.

Around 1900, Einstein added to Newton's theories about gravity and the universe and came up with two major new ideas—his theory of relativity and his concept that mass can be converted to energy. The results were the atomic bomb and what we call atomic power.

Math, you see, is a kind of international language to which pre-historic man, Egyptians, Greeks, Arabs, Europeans—not to mention Chinese and Americans and many others—have all contributed. It's a language of number and measurement that is the backbone, if not the blood and guts, of science. It's a language as stripped of emotion as a language can be. Its beauty lies in its simplicity, believe it or not, and you can get emotional about it only because of its simplicity and because of what it can reveal to you about where we have been, where we are, and where we may be going in this world.

CHAPTER 8

COUNTING, FROM ABACUS TO COMPUTER

The first mathematical statement you ever made was probably in reply to the question, "How old are you?" You held up two little fingers. "I am two," you said as you'd been taught to say. And very likely the statement didn't make a bit of sense to you. Two what? "I am two" was a cute little answer that made your parents proud of you but made no sense to you at all.

If you were lucky when you really began to learn to count, you learned by counting things rather than by a meaningless parroting of words without relationship to things you could see or feel. And when you began to learn to count, you began to learn formal mathematics.

I was fortunate that my mother taught me by having me count such things as forks and spoons, eggs and little chickens. When my father thought I was ready for numbers beyond twenty, he taught me to count things as specific as marbles.

As shepherds had done with stones or pebbles tens of centuries before, my father counted out ten marbles and then started another pile of ten. As I counted after him I soon realized that all I needed to learn was the names for the completed piles of ten marbles—thirty, forty, fifty, sixty, and so on—for I already knew how to count to twenty. To the group names I added one, two, three, and so on up to nine. And how convenient, I thought, that you simply added the sound "tee" to four, six, seven, eight, and nine to get the group names. Nor were the words twenty, thirty, and fifty very different or hard to learn.

After learning that "hundred" was simply a name for a larger group made up of ten small groups of ten, it was easy for me to count to a thousand, which is simply a name for a still larger group made up of ten groups of hundreds.

If man had eight fingers and eight toes, eight or sixteen would likely be the number in the small groups, and sixty-four (eight eights) or two hundred and fifty-six (sixteen sixteens) the number in the next larger groupings. In fact, the number of fingers *and* toes, twenty, was the group number of some peoples, including the Mayas of Mexico.

As you may know, French counting shows signs of grouping by twenties. The French don't have a single word for eighty (eight tens), as we do. Instead, they use a hyphenated word for four twenties *(quartre-vingts).* Nor do they have special words for seventy or ninety. They count from twenty to sixty by tens as we do; then they add numbers from one to twenty to the number for sixty *(soixante).* Likewise, for the numbers from eighty to one hundred, they add their words for from one to twenty to *quatre-vingt* (four twenties with the *s* dropped).

Most groups, however, developed a system of counting based on ten and multiples of ten. When some people changed from being hunters to being herdsmen, they soon found they needed to be able to count to more than just ten or twenty.

As long as a shepherd had only ten or fifteen sheep, he could recognize each animal well enough to know when he had driven them all into a pen or corral at night for protection against wolves or thieves. As flock sizes increased, some brilliant shepherd conceived the idea of letting a small pebble represent a sheep; and as each moved into the pen, he would throw a pebble into a separate pile. When all the flock was driven in, he would have a pebble record of the number of his sheep.

You might be surprised to know that this sort of counting is the origin of our word "calculate." This word for counting comes from the Latin word *calculus,* meaning a counting stone. And *calculus* itself comes from *calx,* a word meaning limestone. So calculating is an ancient word relating to a very important activity of mankind.

No doubt early shepherds soon felt a need for names for numbers beyond twenty. It may even be that they started building small pens to enclose groups of ten sheep. Then all they would have to do was to count and remember the number of penfuls plus a number less than ten. It was a simple step then to give a special name for the penfuls. In English we add the sound "tee" to three, four, five, and so on, and with minor changes we get the group words thirty, forty, fifty, and so on.

It probably wasn't very long before some shepherd thought of using a small stick to represent ten sheep in a pen along with pebbles to represent individual sheep. Imagine his delight when he discovered he could represent as many as ninety-nine sheep with nine sticks and nine pebbles instead of using ninety-nine pebbles. That was real mathematical progress.

Even you or I might have been able to take the next step and invent a word like "hundred" for the name of the number of sheep contained in ten pens. The counting shepherd could represent the new grouping with a longer stick or with a larger stone.

As long as each kind of group was represented by a different symbol—a long stick for a hundred, for instance; a smaller one for ten; and pebbles for units—their position didn't matter much. But it was natural for him to have the pebbles nearest his counting hand, since he would be handling them ten times more often than the stick symbol for ten, and a hundred times more often than his symbol for a hundred.

Soon someone thought of using a counting board. At first, no doubt, he represented numbers of sheep from one to nine by small pebbles; and perhaps he used a different size of pebble for the nine to represent ten, twenty, thirty, and so on; and still another size for the groupings of one hundred. To make it easier for him, he often made grooves in his counting board to slide the pebbles in as he counted.

Once man started using a counting board, it was natural for him to continue the practice of placing the most frequently used symbols closest to his counting hand. If he were right-handed, he would have the small stones representing the units one to nine closest to his hand; stones representing groups of ten, one groove to the left; and stones representing hundreds, two grooves to the left. Thus began the representation of group numbers by position.

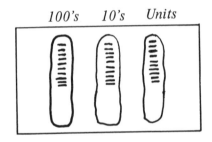

100's   10's   Units

Someone was bound to see that the size of the pebbles didn't really make any difference as long as he considered the stones in the right-hand groove as representing units from one to ten; the ones in the first groove to the left as representing groups of ten; and the ones in the groove two positions to the left as representing groups of a hundred.

Now the way was paved for the introduction of a counting device still used over much of the world—the string and bead abacus. Someone saw that it would be more convenient than a counting board to have counting beads or disks on a string or leather thong stretched on a wooden frame. Besides, the beads were lighter than the pebbles and couldn't be lost as long as the strings were unbroken.

A common form of the abacus consists of four or five strings stretched in a wooden or plastic frame with nine beads on each string.

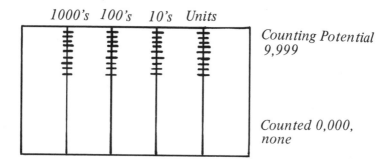

1000's 100's 10's Units

Counting Potential 9,999

Counted 0,000, none

The shepherd with his counting stones and sticks or a counting board would consider the abacus a marvelous invention. For him the beads on the right side could represent individual sheep. The beads on the next string to the left could represent pens filled with ten sheep each; those on the third string, large pens filled with sheep from ten smaller pens. And a bead on the string farthest to his left could represent the sheep it would take to fill ten of the big pens. He would shudder at the thought of having to count that many creatures—unless they were all his!

Let's watch a modern shepherd counting sheep on an abacus. A large, milling flock of sheep is just an ocean of white. So he takes a seat by an opening in a corral so small that sheep have to pass through single file. He signals for the gate to be opened, and with the abacus held about level on his lap, he begins to count.

As the sheep move from the pen of uncounted sheep to the pen for counted sheep, the shepherd uses his right index finger to flip down a bead on the right-hand string for each sheep passing through. "One, two, three, . . . eight, nine. Ah, now," he thinks, "one more and I'll have enough to fill a small pen." So when the tenth sheep passes, he flips away from him all nine of the beads on the right-hand string and flips toward him a bead on the second string from his right.

Then as the eleventh sheep passes he flips down another right-hand bead, and so on until he has flipped all nine toward him. Then as the twentieth sheep passes, he again pushes away from him all nine of these beads and flips toward him a second bead on the second string from his right.

So all the counting from one to ninety-nine sheep takes no more than a quick motion away from him and a motion toward him. It is not until the hundredth sheep passes that he needs to make more movements than this. As the hundredth sheep passes, he flips the nine beads on the right-hand string away from him, sees that there are no more beads on the second string to the left that can come toward him, so flips all nine of them away from him, and slides one on the third string to the left toward him. To an ancient shepherd, this would represent the number of sheep in a pen large enough to hold the sheep from ten smaller pens of ten sheep each.

The shepherd moves a bead toward him on the right-hand string or nine beads away from him every time a sheep passes. He never moves more than one bead toward him on any string for a sheep passing. Once he moves a bead toward him, the counting of that sheep is completed. He moves a bead toward him on the string if all nine on that string have not already been moved toward him. He continues this process going from right to left until he finds a bead he can pull toward him. If he has just counted the nine-hundred and ninety-ninth sheep, all nine beads on the three strings from his right are toward him. As the thousandth sheep passes, he flips away the beads on the unit's string, the nine beads on the ten's string, and the nine beads on the hundred's string, and slides a bead toward him on the fourth string from the left, the thousand's string.

Let's suppose that when the shepherd gets all the sheep on

the counted side of the gate from the uncounted side, his abacus looks like this:

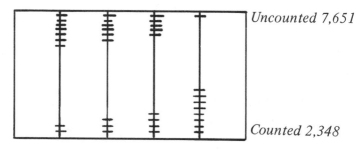

Uncounted 7,651

Counted 2,348

You would probably have little trouble realizing that he has counted two thousand three hundred and forty-eight sheep. Or as a very early shepherd might say, two great big penfuls, three big penfuls, four small penfuls, and eight sheep.

How many sheep would this arrangement on an abacus represent?

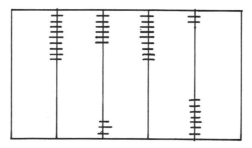

If you answer three hundred and seven, you would probably make a good abacus operator.

Counting itself is a matter of change of position, either the position of your eyes as you count stationary objects or animals, or the position of the animals or objects as they move past your eyes. With the invention of the counting board and abacus, man made size of groups a matter of position too, each string representing groups ten times as large as the size represented by the string on the right and one tenth as large as the size of the groups represented by a string immediately to the left.

So the position left or right on the abacus represents the size of the groups; the number of beads pulled toward the counter on a string represents the number of groups of that size that has been counted. The beads away from the counter represent uncounted or nonexistent objects or things. The beads toward the counter represent objects or things that he has counted. As someone has put it, counting is a matter of objective number (what's "out there" and counted) and subjective position (how the counter has arranged his symbols to represent the number "out there" and counted).

When some men turned from sheepherding to agriculture, they tried to adapt their methods of counting sheep to measurement of distance (line or linear measurement), to size of fields (surface measurement in square units), and to volume (cubical measurement). But we'll go into some of these difficulties in a later chapter.

Man's greatest practical difficulty with numbers came when he first wrote them down. The brilliant Greeks failed completely to introduce a written system to enable them to do the work of the abacus on paper or in the sand. Probably they didn't even conceive the need or convenience of such a system. The Romans did no better. Where the Romans wrote MMCCCXLVIII, the Hindus and Arabs wrote a few centuries later something similar to 8432, since they wrote from right to left. We write 2,348, of course. Imagine trying to do arithmetic with Roman numerals!

It was a Hindu who made a major breakthrough in mathematics by deciding to represent the empty column on the counter's side of an abacus with a symbol. He called it *sunya*, the Hindu word for "empty," and wrote it "." or "0." We call it zero, of course. The Hindus also introduced individual signs for the digits. The sign $=$, representing two, gradually changed to Z, and finally to the Arabic 2; $\equiv$ changed to $\mathbf{3}$ and gradually to 3, for example.

The Arabs introduced the Hindu numerals to Europeans, and today we call them Arabic numerals. Although the Arabs had been using the numerals for centuries, the earliest use of Gobar (or so-called Arabic) numerals in England dates back only to 1490. With what we call Arabic numerals and positional numbering, it was a fairly simple step to introduce decimals; but decimal fractions have been in general use in Europe for less than two centuries, only since the French Revolution. The number 267.569 is read two hundred sixty-seven and five hundred and sixty-nine thousandths, and it means two times one hundred, plus six times ten, plus seven, plus five times one-tenth, plus six times one-hundredth, plus nine times one-thousandth. Aren't Arabic numbers and decimal fractions a wonderful simplification?

Fractions, too, are simply to write with the wonderful Arabic numbers, now part of the international language of mathematics. Instead of three-fourths, we may write simple $\frac{3}{4}$.

With the teaching of Gobar numerals in all the schools of Europe and America, the once-proud abacus was condemned to the nursery for that part of the world. But now, strangely enough, it is being rescued from the nursery to teach students the principle of the electronic digital computer.

The French mathematician, scientist, and philosopher Blaise Pascal invented a mechanical computer back in the seventeenth century. Mechanical computers such as adding machines and cash registers can be constructed to handle our system of tens easily enough. But digital electronic computers work with just two basic symbols, electrical current on and electrical current off, written out 1 and 0.

The shepherd used to an abacus would probably have less trouble understanding the basic principle of the digital computer than most college students. Let's compare an abacus patterned after the digital computer with one the shepherd might be accustomed to using.

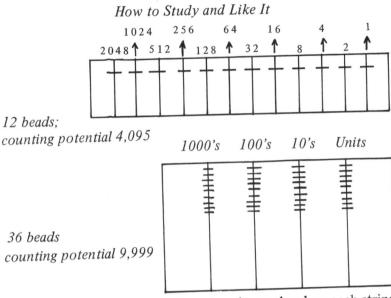

12 beads;
counting potential 4,095

36 beads
counting potential 9,999

In the computer abacus, there is only one bead on each string instead of nine. The second string from the right represents a pen of two sheep instead of a pen of ten. The third string from the right represents a pen of four instead of a pen of a hundred sheep. The fourth string from the right represents a pen of eight instead of a pen of a thousand. In short, each position except the first represents a group twice as large as that represented by the bead on the string to its immediate right. Not more than one group can be represented on any one string.

Now let's watch the shepherd count sheep on this computer-type abacus. As the first sheep comes by, he flips the bead farthest to his right toward him. In computer language the number can be written 000000000001.

When the second sheep passes by, the shepherd flips the right-hand bead away from him and slides the second bead from his right toward him. In computer language the number is written 000000000010.

As the third sheep passes, he again flips the right-hand bead toward him. The written number is 000000000011 in computer language.

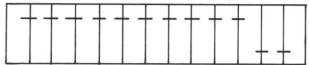

As the fourth sheep passes, the shepherd flips the right-hand bead away from him, sees that the second bead is near him, flips it away also, and flips the third bead from his right toward him. The number is written 000000000100.

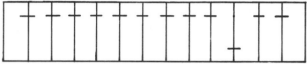

So the right-hand bead is moved every time something is counted; and one bead is always flipped toward him. When this occurs, the movement from right to left ceases and the counting movements are completed. Suppose the shepherd has counted one hundred and eleven sheep. The number would be written 000001101111. His abacus would be arranged like this:

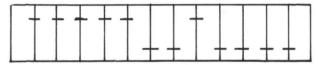

As the one-hundred-and-twelfth sheep passes, he pushes away from him successively from right to left each of the four beads to the right. Then he pulls toward him the fifth bead from the left. One hundred and twelve in computer language is written 000001110000.

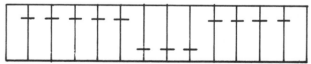

Suppose the shepherd decides he wants to represent one hundred and three on his new abacus. As someone writing a big number with ordinary numbers, he would find the biggest multiple of his number system (two in this case) less than one hundred and three. He finds that the biggest "pen" or group number is $2 \cdot 2 \cdot 2 \cdot 2 \cdot 2 \cdot 2 = 64$. So the seventh bead from his right must come toward him. The next biggest group number less than one hundred and three minus sixty-four is equivalent to 32 in Gobar numerals. So continuing this process, he would arrive at the following arrangement on his abacus, written 000001100111:

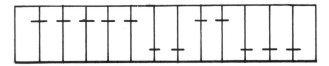

How would you like to try to remember this number in computer notation? It would be rather difficult. Why? Because unless you have made up some words for the group names under the computer, binomial, or two system, the number is nameless. Here you have a good illustration of the importance of giving names to numbers and mathematical operations. You see now how to count using the computer system, but the results would be very hard to remember because you have no names or system of naming the numbers that result in the computer notation. You have to get computer numbers into the familiar Gobar system, just as you have to convert kilometers to miles, before you feel at home with them. We still find the system of tens quite satisfactory for most purposes; but the system of twos has become almost unbelievably important in this age of technology.

Without the system of twos, the modern electronic digital computer would be impossible. And without the electronic digital computer, neither would our modern space and atomic technology be possible. A long history links the shepherd's abacus to the electronic computers, a history that is fascinating all the way.

CHAPTER 9

IT HELPS TO KNOW WHAT YOU'RE TALKING ABOUT,
or
Fractions for College Students

"Do you think you can help me with Math A?" a girl asked me over the phone one Friday, about halfway through the first semester I tutored professionally.

"I should hope so," I replied. "What seems to be your trouble?"

There was a long pause. "It's pretty bad," she said in a quiet voice. "I've forgotten how to use fractions, and I'm too embarrassed to ask the teacher how to do them."

I could scarcely believe my ears. Somebody in a state university who could not handle fractions! Surely, it would be easy to teach them, I thought—especially since I was tutoring a freshman regularly in an engineering math course, and he was now making *A's* on his tests.

"I'll be glad to try to help you," I told the girl, and we made an appointment for early the next week.

After she hung up, I almost wished she hadn't called. How do you teach such fundamentals as dividing or adding fractions? How could a girl reach college with such a dislike for math that she had forgotten or hadn't learned fifth-grade arithmetic? With engineering math students, I'd been able to assume that they had good backgrounds in arithmetic and algebra, and usually in geometry. But how could I prepare myself in one weekend to teach someone to handle fractions?

The only thing I could think to do was to try to remember why I had always liked math and how I'd learned about it. If I could recall clearly why I'd liked math from the start, maybe I could remove some of her dislike. If I could remember how I'd learned fractions, perhaps I could teach her the same way.

I'd found it easy to tutor algebra, trig, and calculus, because I'd had to study those courses by correspondence. To tutor trig, for example, all I needed to do was to present it in the same ways I'd had to look at it in order to understand it for myself.

But dividing and adding fractions was a different matter. It had been a long time since I'd learned about fractions. I had to reach way, way back in my memory to recall my father's teaching me to handle fractions a year or so before I took them up in school. I began to wonder why I'd wanted to learn about fractions and why I'd liked math as far back as I could recall.

Even before I could count to ten, my father had already begun to make lines, angles, and directions mean something to me. He was a farmer; so it was important to him to be able to lay out a field to contain a certain number of acres, especially under the acreage controls started during the Franklin D. Roosevelt administration. It was important to him to be able to calculate how many bushels a granary held when it was full or half full. It was important to him to be able to estimate the number of cubic yards of dirt required to make a small dam. He didn't know much math, but he could use all the math he knew. He wished he knew more, and he made my brother and me *feel* that math was important.

As early as I can remember—I suppose when I was about four—my mother would send me in mid-morning or mid-afternoon to take a jar of water or tea to the field where my father was cultivating cotton or kafir. She would tell me to walk northeast to some knoll or fence corner, and from there I'd be able to see where he was working. While he rested a few minutes, in the shade if he could find any, he would draw pictures in the dirt or sand and show me, for instance, how to draw a perpendicular to a straight line or how to figure out the number of acres in a field.

I didn't always understand what he tried to show me, but I always felt it was important and that I'd be more of a man once I did understand.

I was always amazed at the way my father put his knowledge to use. For example, he never did wear a watch, but by one observation or another he could tell almost exactly what time it was.

I began to notice when I was very young that Dad always got in from the field for the noon meal just as the noon news of the livestock market was coming on. I wondered how he knew when to quit in order to have time to drive the team of mules from the field to the barn, water them, put them in a lot, and get to the house just in time for the noon market news.

"Daddy, how do you know what time to quit work for noon?" I asked one morning after I had taken him a jar of water wrapped in wet burlap to keep it cool.

"My clock tells me," he laughed, patting his stomach.

"No, really, Daddy, how do you do it?" I asked seriously, knowing that he was teasing me.

"It's easy," he said, grinning down at me. "I just look at the shadow of a fence pole. If it's in a north-south fence, when the shadow is in line with the fence, it's about ten minutes after twelve." (We lived in the western part of the time zone.) "So I quit when the shadow is a little to the northwest." He was looking along the fence row as he spoke.

"Look at that little rock," he continued, pointing at a small pebble near a fence pole. "When the shadow gets there, I'll stop and get to the house in time for the market news."

103

I could hardly wait to see if he was right, although certainly I expected him to be. Every few minutes I took out a moment from watching crows, horned toads, grasshoppers—the sort of thing that interests four- and five-year-olds—and went to see how far the shadow had moved. Dad was about a hundred yards from the fence and coming toward it when the shadow reached the pebble.

"It's time to go," I shouted, tossing my straw hat in the air to make sure of catching his attention above the sound of the cultivator blades cutting through the weeds and the red earth.

When he reached the end of the row, he said we'd have to hurry to make it on time. So he hoisted me to the back of Old Pete, one of the mules, cautioned me to hold tight to the harness, and drove faster than usual to the barn, about a quarter of a mile away. He didn't want to miss the news that day because he had calves ready to send to market if prices seemed right.

Sure enough, just as we stepped into the house, his hand on my shoulder, the announcer was switching by remote control to a man at the stockyards. Daddy was really smart, I thought, to be able to figure out time like that.

Dad seemed to take advantage of every opportunity he could to make my brother and me aware of the importance of math. What a delight it was when he showed me how the level worked that he and my brother were using to survey a hillside for terraces. I think he could almost have guessed the proper slope to make the terraces without any surveyor's equipment. But he wanted to be certain, and with the level, he gave my brother and me another lesson in the importance of math.

Dad made sure that we knew the differce between counting and measuring. He said you could be sure about the number of cattle in a lot, at least if you didn't try to count unborn calves as a certain fraction of an animal. But measuring was a different matter: You could be only as accurate as your yardstick or tape measure would allow.

"Somewhere in measuring," he'd say, "you've got to make a

guess at the accuracy." If you were measuring a field, accuracy to the nearest foot was close enough; but if you were measuring a floor for linoleum or a rug, you would want to try to be accurate to the nearest inch.

"There can be exactly ten calves in a pen," he said, "but there can never be a rope *exactly* ten feet long except in someone's imagination." I could see that counting was a much simpler matter than measuring.

Dad also made sure I could count to twenty without a mistake before he'd let me try to count higher for him. "If you know simple math well," he'd say, "a new idea in math may still seem hard at first. But if you don't know the simple parts well, you may find a new idea impossible to learn."

I kept begging Dad to teach me to count to a hundred. So one day after I had counted to twenty perfectly a number of times, he brought several sacks of marbles from town. I counted the marbles after him, and as we reached ten, twenty, thirty, and so on, we would start a new pile of marbles. Presently I realized that all we were doing was reaching the name for a certain number of piles of ten marbles each and adding one, two, three, and so on, to the group name: ". . . twenty-eight,twenty-nine, thirty." A pile was completed, and we started on a new one: "thirty-one, thirty-three . . . thirty-nine, forty."

How easy and simple math is, I thought. Throughout that summer, every time I saw one of my young relatives who didn't know how to count, I had to try to teach him. And two or three of them learned.

Because my father and other relatives had helped satisfy some of my curiosity about direction, time, and numbers, I found arithmetic in the first grades of school quite simple for me. Fortunately, I attended a two-room rural school where the primer and the first four grades were taught by one teacher in a little room. So after I did my arithmetic and other lessons, I'd listen to and watch students in the more advanced grades have their arithmetic lesson with the teacher.

When I was in the third grade, I started noticing pupils talking about fractions. Fifth graders took up fractions, but they were in the big room of the two-room schoolhouse; so I couldn't watch the class of fifth graders recite.

I felt I just had to know about fractions. But my father was a little reluctant to teach me. First he asked my mother to see my report cards. When he noticed that my very best grades were in arithmetic (my teacher was using a number grading system), he said he'd try to teach me.

As I remembered how easy to understand my father had made fractions, I decided that was the way I would try to teach the girl who had called me. Nothing can be made too simple for someone who doesn't understand, I believed.

How frustrating it must be for her to reach college knowing so little about one of the basic tools of civilization—mathematics. I remembered that it was bad enough for me waiting for my father to teach me the secrets of fractions. But I'd been eager to learn. If she didn't remember fractions, she had probably never worked with them confidently and she had probably developed a strong dislike for fractions. How irritating it must be for her to have to try to learn them now.

The more I thought about the problem of teaching the girl to handle fractions, the more I realized that it was going to be a greater challenge to my tutoring ability than to teach trigonometry or calculus. And I was determined not only to teach her to handle fractions but also to give her some awareness of the importance of math in the development of our complicated world of technology.

Right away during her first hour, I found that Suzanne could handle addition, subtraction, multiplication, and division of whole numbers reasonably well. So I didn't think her trouble was with counting, or objective, numbers, the kind of numbers that relate to things that can be separated physically like cows or wagons. The rest of the hour went something like this:

"Do you know how to handle decimals?" I asked Suzanne,

knowing that if she did, her understanding of objective, or counting, numbers was probably adequate for the course she was taking.

"Oh, certainly," she smiled. "You have to know decimals to figure a bank balance, the cost of clothes, and things like that. Yes, I can do decimals," she said, looking at me and probably wondering what my question had to do with fractions.

If Suzanne's trouble was not with objective, or counting, numbers, I knew it must be with her grasp of measuring, or subjective, numbers, the kind of mental numbers that have not yet resulted in physical separations—like acres in a field or yards of cloth in a bolt, for instance. Just as a mule is neither donkey nor horse but a hybrid offspring of the two species, a fraction is neither a counting number nor a measuring number but a kind of offspring of the two. No wonder the fraction has bedeviled millions of people who have failed to recognize the fraction's hybrid character!

Suzanne's trouble was probably not with counting numbers; so I decided to start talking about measuring, or subjective, numbers before introducing her to fractions, the sometimes frightening offspring.

"You're from town," I said, recalling her answers to a few questions I always asked new students of mine. "But you know what a section of land is, don't you?" I asked, sketching a square.

"I think so," she said, wrinkling her forehead. "My father has a farm about three miles out of town. Isn't a section a square block of land a mile on each side, six hundred and forty acres?"

"Right," I replied. "Let's consider for a moment what you've just said. How can a section be *one* section and six hundred and forty acres at the same time?"

She frowned a moment. "Acres are not as big. So I guess a section can be divided into six hundred and forty acres."

"Okay," I agreed. "And what happens when you divide the one-section field into six hundred and forty smaller areas?" I asked.

"You just divide them," she said, wrinkling her brow and squirming in her chair. "I don't see what you're getting at."

"Let me put it this way," I said. "Is the area of the section of land changed at all if we make lines through it to divide it into six hundred and forty one-acre plots?"

"I can't see that it would be," she replied.

"But by dividing, we multiplied, didn't we?" I asked.

"Now, that's ridiculous," she said, looking both perplexed and annoyed.

"I suppose that does need some clarification," I agreed. "You see, we divided the one-section field, but we multiplied the number of fields," I tried to explain.

"Okay," she said, slowly. "I guess I can see that, but I still can't see what you're getting at."

"Well," I said, trying to think of a different approach. "We first mentioned a one-section plot. Then I sketched a square to represent it. Right?"

"Yes," she agreed, none too happily.

"We projected or imagined its existence. In short, we made an object of it. Is this much clear?" I asked.

"Well," she paused. "I guess so."

"Now, you mentioned that a section of land is the same as six hundred and forty acres. To get one-acre plots, how many plots do you divide one section into?" I went on.

"Six hundred and forty, I suppose, but you've got me so confused talking about sections and acres and everything that I'm not sure," she said a little belligerently.

"Six hundred and forty is exactly right," I smiled, hoping to put her a little more at ease. "But let's consider a similar problem we can sketch on paper. Let's take a section, but let's divide it into just two parts," I said, sketching.

"What is the area of each small field?"

"One-half of a section, of course," she said.

"Not really," I replied. "It is completely impossible to divide any real thing *exactly* equally," I tried to explain. "If we had

108

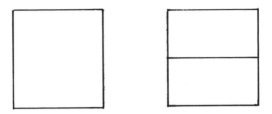

two cows, say, and drove them into separate pens, there would be exactly one cow in each pen; but the cows would still be different, only the number of cows in each pen being the same."

"I can't see what harm it does," Suzanne interrupted, "to pretend we've divided the section exactly in two."

"Good, but we must keep in mind what we are pretending," I said. "You've seen this, haven't you?" I asked, writing $\sqrt{4}$.

"Yes," she said, "we've had that in class. The square root of four is two."

"That's right," I agreed. "That means, for example, if you have a square field four sections in area, each side is two miles long, isn't it?"

"Yes," she said.

"But could you get a field exactly square and exactly two miles on the side, or even two miles on the side to the nearest thousandth of an inch?"

"I don't guess you could very easily, if you put it that way. But we can pretend, can't we?" she asked.

"But if two cows give birth to one calf each, we would have exactly four animals, wouldn't we?" I continued.

"Yes, and I think I can see what you're getting at," Suzanne said.

"Then you shouldn't have as much trouble with the square root of two as the Greeks did," I said, writing $\sqrt{2}$.

"How is that?" she asked, looking at the paper I was writing on.

"You've heard of Pythagoras, the one after whom the theorem is named?" I asked.

"Is that the one that states that the square of the hypotenuse of a right triangle is equal to the sum of the squares of the legs? We had to memorize it for class last week," she replied.

"That's the one," I said. "And there's a legend that Pythagoras and his disciples were traveling from some place to another by ship. One of the disciples figured out that a right triangle whose legs are one unit in length should have a hypotenuse the square-root-of-two units in length. Then another disciple showed that no ordinary fraction or whole number can give two when it is squared. There was a big hullabaloo because, being familiar with cow and sheep numbers and fractions that could be made from them, the Greeks didn't know at first what to do with the square root of two, a subjective or measuring number. So its discoverer was thrown overboard, and the rest of the group was pledged to secrecy!"

"If I'd discovered it, I'd probably have jumped overboard before I told anyone about it," Suzanne laughed.

"Well, the Pythagoreans were confusing cow numbers with lengths. We can get a length the square-root-of-two miles long as accurately as we can get a length a mile long," I said, sketching.

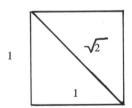

"If we had a perfectly flat area of a perfect square having sides exactly one mile long, the distance from one corner of the square to the opposite one would be exactly the square-root-of-two miles. But of course we can only pretend such accuracy, don't you see?" I asked.

"I think I see," she said.

"It's very important to realize when you are relating numbers to reality and when you are pretending and playing the math game by its rules. It could have saved at least one Greek from getting wet or worse, and it could save a lot of students from——"

"From something worse than a wetting," she interrupted, grinning.

"Okay, then let's get back to the section of land that we're pretending to cut into exactly two equal parts," I went on, sketching again.

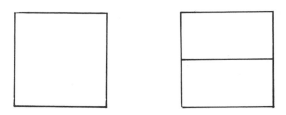

"What is the area of the halves?" I asked.

"One-half of a section, of course," she replied.

"And how do you write it?"

She wrote ½.

"So you'd say that fractions are a matter of position, wouldn't you?" I queried.

She pondered a moment. "Yes, I'd say so," she agreed.

"What does the one refer to?" I asked.

"To a half-section, maybe?" she replied, wrinkling her brow.

"Well, yes," I said hesitantly. "Or we could read this *one section divided by two.* That would make the one refer to the one section, you see, and then the two would refer to?"

"The number of parts after the division," she said confidently.

"Fine," I agreed. "Now suppose a farmer decides to give each of his children three-sixteenths of a section of his one-section farm and to retire on the remainder smaller than a child's share. How many children does he have and how does the area he retires on compare in size to a child's share?"

"You'll have to repeat that," Suzanne said.

After I had repeated the problem a couple of times, she admitted that she didn't know how to do it without a sketch. "Then sketch it," I suggested.

She sketched,

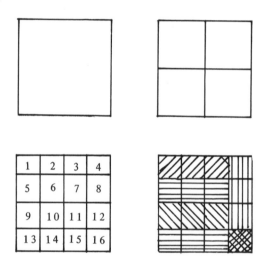

"So," she concluded, "five children could each have three-sixteenths of a section, and the father could retire on an area one-third as large as each child's share."

"Let's think about what you've just done," I suggested. "You've taken the one section you sketched, and first of all you decided to divide it into sixteen parts, didn't you?"

"Yes," she agreed readily.

"What is the area of one of the parts?" I asked.

112

"One-sixteenth of a section, approximately," she said.

She wrote 1/16.

"The one refers to the square object you sketched which represents a section of land as you might see it outlined from the air by roads or fences. The one, then, is an objective number, isn't it?" I queried.

"Uhhh, I guess you could call it that," she admitted, looking slightly puzzled.

"The sixteen refers to the number of parts you decided to divide the object into before you started the divisions, and you knew that however hard you tried you couldn't make the parts exactly one-sixteenth of the section. Right?"

"I'd agree to that," she said.

"But by measuring, estimating, or pretending to measure, you were determined to divide the object into sixteen nearly equal parts. So the sixteen is a measuring, or subjective, number. Agreed?"

"I can't disagree with that," she said, nodding her head as if she were following the line of thought.

"What happened when you actually made the divisions?" I asked.

"I just made them," she said with a shrug.

"Well, didn't you get objects you could count? In fact, you put numbers in the little squares. Didn't you change from subjective number in your mind to objective number on the paper?"

"I think I see what you're getting at," she smiled a little uncertainly.

"Now, after you got the section divided into *approximate* sixteenths, you could count them off three at a time, couldn't you?" I asked.

"That's what I did, wasn't it?"

"So the three, or numerator of the three-sixteenths, is the counting, or objective, part of the fraction to start with, and the sixteenths is the subjective part."

113

"Sounds pretty reasonable," she agreed.

"But you couldn't use the three until you had made the subjective sixteen objective—that is, on the paper. Right?"

"Right," she agreed, "and then I just divided the sixteen parts into threes as if I were dividing whole numbers." She beamed as she spoke.

"Excellent, and what *was* an objective three has *become* a subjective or divisor three!" I added, feeling pretty good for the first time about tutoring fractions. And to drive home the point about making the subjective objective I drew a parallel.

"Were you ever afraid of the bogey-man, devil, or whatever it was your parents may have threatened you with sometimes for being naughty when you were a child?"

Suzanne laughed, admitting that she had been. "Sometimes I've felt the same way toward fractions!" she exclaimed.

"Well, I think this rather vague evil we are sometimes threatened with as children scares us, both because it is vague and indefinite and because it supposedly has many names and locations. We have trouble objectifying it so we can consider it with less fear," I went on.

"Are you suggesting that I have to learn how to objectify fractions, as I was just doing in the sketch?" Suzanne asked.

"I was trying to suggest that it would be a great help," I agreed, "and I was also trying to make another point. How old were you the first time you can remember hearing a preacher discuss the devil or bogey-man as Satan?"

"Oh, I was about ten or eleven, I guess," she replied.

"Did your preacher describe him as a fallen angel?" I asked.

"Yes, I believe he did," she agreed.

"Didn't the bogey-man seem much less frightening now that you had a nice specific name like Satan for him and now that he was a good deal more specific?"

"Come to think of it, the devil never seemed so scary after I learned the name Satan for him—or it," she laughed.

"It's the fears we have no names for that affect us most," I said. "Once we can objectify them by giving them a name or describing them or getting them on paper so we can work with them, we become much less afraid of them. We have some idea of how to get busy and do something about objects. Nameless fears tend to paralyze us, but when we give them a name they lose much of their terror. I hope fractions are going to be the same way for you," I said seriously.

"Maybe they will be," Suzanne said hopefully.

"Getting back to your sketch," I said, "isn't what you did like saying that if you divide a section into parts three-sixteenths of a section in area, you get five such parts with a remaining part just one-third as large as the other parts?" I asked.

She frowned a moment and then nodded her agreement.

"Couldn't we write this, then?" I asked, writing,

$$1 \div \frac{3}{16} = 5\frac{1}{3}.$$

"It looks true," Suzanne said, "but I don't see how you got it."

"Watch, then," I said, writing,

$$1 \div \frac{3}{16} = 1 \cdot \frac{16}{3} = 5\frac{1}{3}.$$

"We have made the subjective part of the divisor objective and the objective part subjective," I explained.

"I see!" she exclaimed. "So that's how that inversion comes in that the teacher keeps talking about. You just invert and multiply."

"Suppose a developer buys a half section of land and decides to break it up into country estates one sixty-fourth of a section in area. How many estates could he sell?" I asked.

"I suppose you would divide one-half by one sixty-fourth," she replied.

"Like this?" I asked, writing,

$$\frac{1}{2} \div \frac{1}{64}.$$

"Yes, but both are fractions now. So what do you do?" she asked.

"What did we do a moment ago when we divided one number by another?" I pleaded, shaking my head with discouragement.

"Inverted the number that we were dividing into the other one and multiplied," she said, brightening a little.

"Then please do it," I said.

"I'll try," she responded, writing,

$$\frac{1}{2} \div \frac{1}{64} = \frac{1}{2} \cdot \frac{64}{1} = \frac{64}{2} = 32.$$

"Fine," I said. "Do you see clearly, then, that when an arithmetic problem says divide a number by another, you simply invert the divisor, or number you are dividing by, and multiply?"

"I think so," she said.

"Just one more example, and if you follow it all right, we'll stop belaboring inversions for a while," I promised, thinking how much easier it was to tutor calculus than to tutor fractions. "But we are dealing here with an idea that's basic to all the math you take," I insisted.

"Suppose a rancher has three and a half sections of pasture land and he wishes to divide them into pastures three-eighths of a section in area. How many pastures does he get?"

By now Suzanne's resistance must have been worn down and she must have preferred to accept "inversion" than to fight it any longer. Anyway, after asking if three and a half sections was the same as seven halves, she wrote,

$$\frac{7}{2} \div \frac{3}{8} = \frac{7}{2} \cdot \frac{8}{3} = \frac{7}{\cancel{2}} \cdot \frac{\cancel{8}^{4}}{3} = \frac{28}{3} = 9\frac{1}{3}.$$

"What does the nine and a third mean?" I asked a little wearily.

116

It Helps to Know What You're Talking About

"I guess nine pastures of the size the rancher wants and enough land left over for another one-third the size of the others," she ventured, nodding her head and making me feel that the light was really beginning to dawn.

We then went back to a consideration of the divisions of a section into one-acre patches. This time Suzanne saw fairly quickly that this kind of division could be done with conventional arithmetic. I thought, though, that she still found a little hard to swallow the idea that if you divide one section of area by an area of one six-hundred-fortieth of a section, you get six hundred and forty *fields*.

Multiplying fractions hadn't bothered Suzanne much. But by making sketches she got a better grasp of what it means to multiply two-thirds by four-fifths, for example:

$$\frac{2}{3} \cdot \frac{4}{5} = \frac{8}{15}.$$

She saw that by the rules of arithmetic all that was necessary was to multiply the numerators, or upper parts of the fractions, together and to multiply the denominators, or lower parts of the fractions, together.

With a few more sketches, she began to realize that when both numerator and denominator of a fraction are multiplied by the same value, the size indicated by the fraction does not change:

$$\frac{2}{3} = \frac{2}{3} \cdot 1 = \frac{2}{3} \cdot \frac{4}{4} = \frac{8}{12} \; ; \frac{2}{3} \cdot \frac{5}{5} = \frac{10}{15}.$$

$$\frac{4}{5} = \frac{4}{5} \cdot \frac{2}{2} = \frac{8}{10} \; ; \frac{4}{5} = \frac{4}{5} \cdot \frac{3}{3} = \frac{12}{15}.$$

Soon, she came to see that

$$\frac{2}{3} + \frac{4}{5} = \frac{2(5) + 4(3)}{15} = \frac{10 + 12}{15} = \frac{22}{15}.$$

was simply a slight shortcut for

$$\frac{2}{3} + \frac{4}{5} = \frac{2}{3} \cdot \frac{5}{5} + \frac{4}{5} \cdot \frac{3}{3}$$

$$= \frac{10}{15} + \frac{12}{15} = \frac{22}{15}.$$

Suzanne was puzzled for a moment by the fact that five times two-thirds is the same as two-thirds times five, but that five divided by two-thirds does not equal two-thirds divided by five. But by sketching she saw that rules of inversion held for the divisions:

$$5 \div \frac{2}{3} = 5 \cdot \frac{3}{2} = \frac{15}{2}.$$

$$\frac{2}{3} \div 5 = \frac{2}{3} \div \frac{5}{1} = \frac{2}{3} \cdot \frac{1}{5} = \frac{2}{15}.$$

After she tried a few more problems successfully, Suzanne began to nod her head. "I think I'm beginning to really understand at last the reason for the rule, '*When you divide, invert the divisor and multiply.*'"

"I don't mind shortcuts," she went on, "but I must make sense of them, or I have all sorts of mistakes when I try to use them. I think I understand fractions now, though, don't you?" she asked, glancing directly at me.

"I think so," I said. "And what else have you learned?" I asked.

She frowned thoughtfully a moment, leaning back in her chair. "Two things, I'd say. If I ask myself a lot of questions and make the questions simple enough, the answers are fairly easy to see. And it sure helps me to understand when I make sketches—and make the problem halfway practical," she added.

"You've made it fairly easy so far," I said. "You probably expected me to have all the answers, but instead I've asked most of the questions, and you've provided most of the answers!" I laughed.

"That's okay as long as I understand," she said. "Learning to ask the right questions—and a lot of them—seems to be the main thing."

"And I suppose that's the hardest thing to get in the habit of doing," I added. "But I think you're off to a good start now. Just to make sure, though, why don't we take a look at a few of the problems at the end of your chapter on fractions," I suggested.

"Fine," she agreed, flipping pages to that part of her textbook. Although there were some letter values like *a* and *b* and *x* and *y* involved, Suzanne worked several problems with just a few mistakes; and these were in addition or multiplication of whole numbers. I didn't know whether she would want any more tutorial help now that she had learned to handle fractions.

About a week later, though, Suzanne called me and set up regular twice-a-week appointments for the rest of the semester. If we got all the points that were bothering her cleared up before an hour was up, I'd give her some idea about how long it took for man to discover ideas that now even second graders take for granted. Gradually she began to catch up on fundamentals and to understand better what her teacher was saying about elementary algebra. More to her amazement than to mine, she made a *C* on the final examination, pulling her semester grade up from an *F* to a *D*.

Suzanne was careless with arithmetic and sometimes slow to grasp things. She was quick to admit that. But she was willing to work, willing to admit to herself and to me, at least, when she didn't understand something, and willing to learn, relearn, and review fundamentals. The next semester, with less help from me, she made almost as many *B*'s as *C*'s on tests in intermediate algebra, and she just missed getting a *B* in the course.

It was just as much an accomplishment for Suzanne to make the grades she did as it was for the freshman engineering math student of mine to receive an *A* the first semester. And I was equally proud of the two, for I felt that both had developed good attitudes toward math and that both had done nearly the best they were capable of doing at the time.

As I have learned more about the history of mathematics, I have realized how fortunate I was that my learning retraced the first part, at least, of the path that man had blazed in developing his mathematical knowledge. What a relief it often is even for students like Suzanne to realize that geometry, algebra, or calculus were not handed suddenly to man and that most people are capable of learning and enjoying far more of the wonderful world of mathematics than they expose themselves to.

CHAPTER 10

LISTENING TO THE PROBLEM,
or
The Solution to Equations

In solving equations I have never stopped applying a little rule that I discovered for myself early in the second-semester of elementary algebra. The rule is *Listen to the problem and invert.*

I say I discovered it for myself, because the inversion idea in math is well over a thousand years old. In fact, algebra was developed by the Arabs, who learned to listen partly because Mohammed forbade them the use of pictures.

Algebra, unlike geometry, deals with concepts that are fairly easy to put into words. If you've ever tried it, you know that it's much simpler to explain an algebra problem over the phone than it is to explain a geometric construction or a geometric proof.

The developers of algebra put very little trust in what they saw. The vast deserts over which they traveled offered few nearby visual reference points. Soon they learned not to trust the desert mirages that promised a lake or an oasis but turned out to be only acres more of trackless sand.

The Arabs well knew that sight could be deceptive. They probably would not have been much surprised by an important discovery that scientists studying the eye were to make several hundred years later: The image that strikes the retina, the back of the eye, is actually turned upside down and reversed right to left. That is, the lens of the eye inverts the image. Only by feeling and hearing do we learn to live with the illusion that we are seeing right side up!

Just as the lens of the eye inverts the light striking it, in a sense the Arabs learned to "invert" what they heard in solving equations. Today we learn to invert what we see in order to arrive at a solution of an equation.

When we look at this arrangement of the signs of arithmetic:

$$X$$
$$+ = -$$
$$\div$$

what strikes the retina of our eyes is this pattern:

$$\div$$
$$- = +$$
$$X$$

The multiplication and division signs are inverted upside down, and the plus and minus signs are inverted left to right by the converging lens of the eye, somewhat like this:

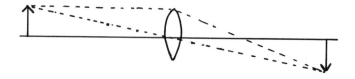

Listening to the Problem

But, I learned all this later. I suppose I wasn't bright enough to see without the help of a teacher that, just as I'd learned to invert in dividing fractions, I had to apply an inversion principle to the solution of equations.

I had to "learn" myself, as they sometimes say in Oklahoma, not teach myself, the principle of listening to the problem and inverting. Sometimes I think *to learn* ought to be acceptable, as it once was, in the sense of "to teach by asking questions a person can answer for himself." I wonder whether you can really *teach* anyone anything. I think teaching may be mainly a matter of helping someone learn for himself.

Anyway, in studying algebra without a teacher, I had to learn by myself or teach myself, however you want to look at it. I soon ran into trouble, as you can well imagine. But it was out of this trouble that I learned for myself the rule *Listen to the problem and invert.*

Suppose you want very much to do a set of algebra problems. Suppose you have filled a half dozen pages with numbers, and have had to sharpen your pencil a couple of times, and still all the solutions are not coming through. Suppose, too, that you won't be able to find out how to solve the set of problems in class tomorrow or next week—because you won't be going to class tomorrow or next week. Suppose, finally, that you have no one to turn to for help, and that you wouldn't even consider turning in a correspondence study lesson with a note admitting that you couldn't do it.

What would you do? I don't think you would give up. Not when you've decided to finish high school by correspondence study and have made all your plans accordingly.

I think you would do just as I did. You might frown, grit your teeth, even say a few of your worst swear words. Despairing, you might even pray a little. Then, when things looked blackest and most hopeless, you'd determine to read aloud and copy the examples once again, the old last-ditch try, to see if a little light might dawn of its own accord. Chances are,

123

it would!

That's how it was when I made my biggest *personal* discovery about algebra. No, I wasn't solving a new theorem or anything of that sort.

I'd been trying to work all the problems by examples, and some just didn't seem to fit the pattern. Then, at my blackest moment, when I felt most tormented about the whole thing, I decided to work my way slowly through the examples a third time.

I copied down an example and said it to myself, with the idea that seeing it *and* saying it *and* writing it ought to do more good than any one by itself. Suddenly the idea came to me that maybe I had been trying too hard to force problems into the pattern of the examples. Reworking them, I could almost guess what step was coming next. Why not take it easier, I thought, and try to let each problem tell *me* what to do?

That is how I learned the math rule that has meant most to me: *Listen to the problem and invert.*

Do you want to hear—not see, hear—what I am talking about? Let me start off with what may appear to you a ridiculously easy problem. But we can understand principles best when the examples are least complicated.

Take *3x=15,* for example. When I learned to listen to a problem of this sort, I learned that the *3* that multiplies the *x* is really saying—and this is the mysterious thing about it— "Have a little mathematical faith and do just the opposite. Don't multiply, divide!" An inversion, if you please. The *3* that multiplies, then, tells me to do the inverse operation of multiplication to both sides of the equation. That is, divide both sides by *3*:

$$3x = 15 \; ; \; \frac{3x}{3} = \frac{15}{3} = 5 \; ; \; x = 5.$$

As all magicians know, seeing can be deceiving! We see sharply only in the center of our vision, the *fovea centralis* or yellow spot, and the sleight-of-hand artists are skilled in directing the center of our vision and attention away from the points where the deception takes place.

Although we see sharply only in the *fovea centralis,* we hear well over our entire range of hearing. We see only in part, but we hear as a whole. If we look at a word to see how it is spelled, for instance, we look at a letter at a time. But if we try to spell from hearing it, we take the whole word and break it down first into syllables and finally into letters. You can see what I mean by considering the word "Colorado," for example.

Seeing, then, is really a kind of addition, and hearing is a kind of division. Multiplication is simply repeated addition *(3x2=2+2+2),* and division is repeated subtraction *(14 ÷ 4=14-4-4-4=2; 14 ÷ 4 = 3 2/4).* The quotient is the number of times that the divisor can be subtracted.

As far as seeing what to do, mathematically speaking, seeing is deceiving—not believing. "Faith cometh from hearing the word." If we believe that we should do the inverse, or opposite, of what we see, faith leads to the solution of our equations.

As obvious as the solution of *3x=15* may seem to you, I have tutored students in college algebra who were still playing the childish guessing game of asking, "Three times what equals fifteen?" Instead of inverting, they were multiplying their guesses by three. You can arrive at the correct solution to *3x=15* in a guess or two, but when a problem is a little more complicated, it is very difficult to arrive at the answer by such a process.

Even the most difficult equations you have to do will usually *tell you* how to solve them, if you will listen for a whisper from the problem to tell you what to do next.

Take $\frac{x}{5}+7=21$, as an example of a slightly more difficult problem than our first one. You can listen to the 7 first or to the 5 first; it doesn't matter. Suppose you listen to the 7. The problem says *plus* seven. But you remember that the *plus* seven is telling you to subtract seven from both sides. So you have

$$\frac{x}{5} + 7 - 7 = 21 - 7,$$

or, anticipating the result, you could have written,

$$\frac{x}{5} = 14$$

Anyway, that would have been the next step.

You have almost reached the solution, but you see that *14* is not equal to *x* but is one fifth of *x*. So you have to listen to the *5* and its position. You see that it's dividing the *x*; so it's really telling you to multiply both sides by *5*, for as you know multiplication is the opposite or inverse of division. So,

$$5 \cdot \frac{x}{5} = 5 \cdot 14;$$

$$\frac{5}{5} x = 70 \; ; x = 70.$$

Or taking the same problem, $\frac{x}{5} + 7 = 21$, you could have listened to the *5* first. Seeing that the *5* is dividing the *x*, you know it's telling you to multiply every term of both sides by *5:*

$$5 \cdot \frac{x}{5} + 5 \cdot 7 = 5 \cdot 21;$$

$$x + 35 = 105.$$

Now seeing the *plus 35,* you know that it's telling you to subtract *35* from both sides, as before:

$$x + 35 - 35 = 105 - 35 \; ; x = 70.$$

Suppose you have *6x - 10 = 2x + 14.* You have to keep in mind that your goal is to have *x* by itself equal to some value or number. That means you have to get all the terms containing *x* on one side (usually you get them on the left) and all the terms not containing *x* on the other. So what does the *plus 2x* on the right side tell you?

It tells you to do the inverse operation; that is, subtract, in this case. So you subtract *2x* from both sides.

$$6x - 2x - 10 = 2x - 2x + 14;$$

$$4x - 10 = 14.$$

Now, of course, the *minus 10* tells you to add *10* to both sides,

$$4x - 10 + 10 = 14 + 10; \quad 4x = 24.$$

What does the *4* that multiplies the *x* tell you to do? To divide both sides by *4*, of course,

$$\frac{4}{4} x = \frac{24}{4}; x = 6.$$

It may well be that you've done these simple operations for years. But considering them as we have here, isn't it clearer to you why people who otherwise seem quite intelligent may have trouble with algebra?

Your eye sees a plus sign, for instance, but you have to listen to hear a minus, too. Your eye sees a division, and you have to hear "multiply." Your eye sees an unknown *x* being multiplied, and you have to hear "divide." Your eye sees a minus sign, and you have to hear "add."

Suppose you have the problem, *ax + bx = c*, and you are to solve for *x*. Having studied examples and having learned to listen to the problem, you see that *x* is multiplied by both *a* and *b*, separately, and you hear the problem tell you to "factor out" (that is, let *x* be multiplied by a single quantity in parenthesis). So you write,

$$x (a + b) = c$$

127

Factoring, you understand, is the inverse operation of "multiplying out."

Now you see that x is multiplied by the quantity $(a + b)$. With enough practice, you divide without even thinking "divide" on a conscious level. You write,

$$\frac{x(a+b)}{(a+b)} = \frac{c}{a+b}, \text{ or simply, } x = \frac{c}{a+b},$$

and that is your answer.

As I advanced through elementary and intermediate algebra by correspondence study, I found that solutions of equations almost invariably involve inversion processes. Not only did I learn to hear *add* when I saw *minus,* multiply when I saw *divide,* subtract when I saw *plus,* and divide when I saw *multiply,* but I also learned to square when I saw a square root sign $\sqrt{\ }$ and take the square root when I saw a factor squared, such as x^2.

When I enrolled in college, such habits of thought about algebra and a systematic plan of attacking geometric proofs and statement problems permitted me to make an entrance score high enough for me to be exempted from a further math requirement. But I decided to take two semesters of physics to meet the physical science requirement for the degree I was seeking, and trigonometry was required for enrollment in physics. Math courses were not usually taught in rooms accessible to a student in a wheelchair. So rather than have special provisions made for me, I took trigonometry by correspondence during the summer before I enrolled in physics.

As in algebra, I found that solutions to trigonometric problems always involved some kind, often the same kind, of inversion steps. Each of the six trigonometric functions, for example, has its inverse or reciprocal. In trig, I learned to think of the division line as an inverter. When a trig function that is a factor crosses a division line, it becomes its inverse or reciprocal. Sine A, for instance, becomes its inverse, cosecant A, in the following step:

128

$$\frac{1}{\text{sine A } (1 + \tan A)} = \frac{\text{cosecant A}}{1 + \tan A} \cdot$$

After I received two degrees from college and began tutoring, I took courses in the differential and integral calculus by correspondence study. Still without a teacher other than myself, I found again that as long as I followed the practice of *seeing* one process and *hearing* in my mind's ear the instruction to do the inverse operation, I had little trouble solving the calculus equations.

The process of integration in the calculus is even called the inverse of differentiation. And the process of differentiation is naturally called the inverse of integration. As far as I have been able to learn, all solutions of equations involve the processes of inversion in one way or another.

I have found that when students of the calculus have trouble it is usually not with the basic concepts of the calculus but with the inversion processes of trigonometry! Solutions of equations, then, involve seeing one operation and hearing (or thinking) and doing the inverse.

If you like, then, you can think of the equal sign as a sort of lens. When the *3* of *3x = 15* passes through the equal sign from left to right, it changes its position, and it changes its nature from objective number to subjective number, from multiplier to divisor: $x = \frac{15}{3} = 5$.

If you have *x + 7 = 10,* then as the plus 7 passes through the equal sign, it becomes minus *7,* and you have *x = 10-7 = 3.*

Whether you see an inversion or hear it, the process is the same. But if you see the equal sign as a sort of lens, you must remember that only the position of the multiplier or divider is inverted, and only the sign of terms added or subtracted is changed.

Beware of the mistake many students make when they have a problem of the type *3x = 15.* Too often they write, *incorrectly,*

$$3x = 15; \quad x = \frac{15}{-3},$$

because they have inverted both position and sign simultaneously. The frequency of this kind of error has caused me to emphasize "listening inversion" as I learned it first and as I presented it first in this chapter, rather than "seeing inversion"—at least when it comes to solutions of equations.

The rules for listening to problems, then, are these:
1) A plus sign suggests that you subtract.
2) A minus sign suggests that you add.
3) Multiplication suggests that you divide.
4) Division suggests that you multiply.
5) Terms "multiplied out" suggest that you factor.
6) Factored terms suggest that you may need to multiply out.
7) A square root sign $\sqrt{}$ suggests that you square.
8) A term squared suggests that you prepare to take the square root.

Whatever is happening in the original equation, then, suggests the inverse operation, its opposite. As Euler, the great German mathematician, kept telling his students: "Invert. Invert. Invert!"

I don't pretend that these rules can be followed blindly, that they are all you need to know to solve any algebraic equation. But I do insist to you, first, that they can help you understand better any example solution given and, second, that they can help get you started toward a solution. You can't solve any equation until you try.

The more you think about this mysterious process of inversion, the more you realize that it may be one of the principles of life itself. It is a principle of photography and printing. Take the negative of a black and white picture, for example. Where the picture is dark, the negative is light, and *vice versa.* The face of the type that makes a *B* is the converse. ᗺ Out of apparent evil, good sometimes comes, if people have

130

the faith and the will to "invert" as they adapt or react to it.

For fun sometimes, try to see how many proverbs you can think of that reflect the principle. Here are a couple to start you off: "Every cloud has a silver lining," and "After the darkest hour comes the dawn." I'll leave you for now with another one that's pertinent to the solution of equations: "To understand and solve any problem, you must *turn it over in your mind* and act upon it."

CHAPTER 11

EUCLID INVERTED:
Seeing behind Mathematical Proofs

It's intriguing that the inversion principle keeps reappearing and keeps helping to simplify math. I first ran into it by name, without really appreciating what the name meant, when I learned fractions. I met it again in the solution of equations. You'd think that from then on I would be on the alert for inversion.

But I had quite a struggle with geometry before some struggles with algebra helped me realize that Euclid's formal proof is simply the inversion of the inductive reasoning that should precede it. (You'll soon see what I mean.)

Geometry is really just a kind of back flip of algebra. If you can turn it over one way, you can turn it over the other way, too. Geometry appeared before algebra in the history of math, but it could have inverted either way.

Because I studied elementary algebra before geometry, for me, at least, geometry was like an inversion of algebra. As we've discussed it, algebra was developed by a people who were aural-minded. For me and most people, the problem is to visualize algebra problems, particularly those expressed in words. In doing geometric proofs, the problem is just the reverse: to relate the words of postulates and theorems to the lines and figures.

I suppose it's rather natural for a person to have a little trouble learning to see behind the deductive proofs of Euclid, the logical, step-by-step proofs, from the given conditions to the conclusion desired. For one thing, it has been said that "Euclid's problems are nice problems, but they exist in a void." They are like a filament in a light bulb: it generates light, but it's impossible to get into the void with it.

As I see it now, the problem with Euclid is that there's no apparent place in his neat, deductive proofs for us to get inside. There seems to be no personal viewpoint *until* we *invert* the deductive proof and can look into the problem and divide it into manageable parts. You have to find meaningful reference points, as the following story shows.

Around 1890, the story goes, a group of cowboys was riding along a stretch of prairie in the Cheyenne-Arapaho lands of what is now western Oklahoma. As far as the eye could see, even from the back of a horse, there were no recognizable landmarks.

Suddenly ahead of them the cowboys noticed an Indian jumping as high as he could above the tall buffalo grass, looking first in one direction and then in another. Obviously unhappy with himself, he pretended to ignore the approaching riders.

Noisily, the cowboys rode up to within a few feet of the lone Cheyenne. "Hey, Indian," one of them shouted, "you lost?"

The Cheyenne straightened up to his full height and looked coldly at his tormentors. "Me no lost," he grunted. "Teepee lost. Me here!"

The Cheyenne had the essential characteristics of a good math and science student. He was interested in finding other things in relationship to himself. And he knew that the only meaningful starting point was the exact location of himself, for which he had to have reference points.

Less than seventy years later, a young chief of the same Indian tribe had mastered enough math and science to pilot one of the Marine Corps' hottest jet fighters. And not only this, in competition with graduates of Annapolis and some of the best universities in the United States, he was selected as Cadet of the Week at Pensacola for his excellence both in flying and in class work.

Like his fellow tribesman of an earlier era, Lawrence Hart had learned to locate himself, not just in relation to a teepee, but in relation to math and science as well. Valedictorian of Hammon High School, my home school, he had managed to see behind Euclid and to realize that the trick of mathematical proofs and statement problems lies in getting a personal viewpoint into the problem.

The trouble with Euclid and his *Elements,* and with most of the Greek mathematicians, who were primarily visually oriented, is that they present only one side of their reasoning. They give us logical steps in their proofs, but they don't show us *how* they decided on the steps in the first place. The trouble with a lot of present-day authors of math and science textbooks is that they go back to the same ancient error.

Euclid presented neat, polished solutions to problems that the Egyptians had known how to solve, in some cases, for hundreds of years. His solutions are dress-up versions, suggesting little of the sweat that went into ironing the problems out. The Greeks considered math mainly as a way *to refine the mind.*

But perhaps you want to learn a little math to make money as an engineer, or just to work off some requirements that you've been struggling with. Had you and I been in one of Euclid's classes, we might have fared little better than one of his students who asked at the end of his first lesson in geometry what he would get by learning such things. Euclid looked at him with great indignation and called to his slave, "Give him a penny since he must needs make gain by what he learns."

Fortunately, the discoverer of analytic geometry was interested in revealing not only the fruit of his ideas but the methods whereby he got them. In his *Rules for the Direction of the Mind,* (*c.* 1637), Descartes wrote that some of the ancient Greeks, such as Euclid, seemed to present their proofs "in order to win our admiration for their achievements rather than to disclose to us that method itself which would have annulled the admiration accorded." In short, Descartes said that the ancient Greek mathematicians were inclined to show off instead of show how.

But I didn't know all this when I started studying geometry by correspondence for high-school credit. I went over and over and over the proofs and explanations, until it dawned upon me that the Euclidean proof left *me* out!

My textbook called it formal proof, and I was beginning to think it was too formal for a farm boy like me. But I wasn't inclined to give up without a real struggle. The proofs looked fine; I could follow them step by step. But I just couldn't seem to develop similar proofs in the exercises I was assigned.

I would go over Proposition 1, draw the lines, write the "givens," the statements of the proof, and the reasons. Then I'd try to do the assignment. I'd frown and shake my head and go back and run through the proposition again, reading everything aloud. I'd think maybe I had the pattern, and then I'd go back to the assigned problems again. Same result.

This went on for an entire afternoon. I even reviewed all the previous axioms and postulates half a dozen or so times, trying to visualize them as I said them to myself. Finally I decided to forget the assignment until the next day. But I must have really impressed Proposition 1 on my mind, because that night I dreamed of lines, definitions, proofs, and reasons.

The next day I was eager to get started again. I'd considered arithmetic and algebra as my best subjects. It irritated me when I had trouble with any kind of math problem, and I usually struggled with a troublesome problem until I generated enough light to see into it and see what was going on.

Filled with a strange mixture of eagerness and dread, I tackled my geometry again. I moved step by step through Proposition 1 with all the concentration I could muster. I copied the proposition and said to myself:

"When two straight lines intersect, the vertical angles thus formed are equal."

I drew the figure:

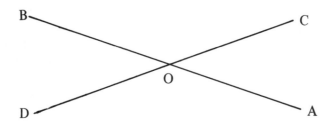

I wrote down the given: "Given: Straight lines *AB* and *CD* intersecting at O and forming vertical angles *AOC* and *BOD*." And I wrote the statement to be proved: "Prove: Angle *AOC* equals angle *BOD*."

Then I started to write the statements and reasons of the proof:

Statements	**Reasons**
1. *AB* and *CD* are straight lines.	1. Given.
2. Angles *AOB* and *COD* are straight angles.	2. A straight angle is an angle whose sides lie on the same straight line and extend in the opposite direction from the vertex.

That much I accepted.

3. Angle *AOB* equals angle *COD*.
4. Angle *COB* equals angle *COB*.
5. Therefore angle *AOC* equals angle *BOD*.

3. All straight angles are equal.
4. Identity.
5. If the same quantity is subtracted from two equal quantities, the remainders are equal.

The fifth step made me think a little. I saw that if angle *COB* was subtracted from angle *AOB*, angle *AOC* remained; and that if angle *COB* was subtracted from angle *COD*, angle *BOD* remained. Angles *AOC* and *BOD* appeared equal, but I had to think about the reason in Step 5, even though I'd memorized the axiom. Finally I remembered that if two boys of about equal size and position got off a seesaw, the board would still be in balance. Nodding my head, I accepted that reason, too.

Again I returned to a proof I was assigned, and I closed my eyes and recited practically all of the previous axioms and postulates, hoping to think of what I'd need to do for my proof. Nothing occurred to me. I rubbed my forehead and slapped my left hand hard to the back of my head. "Why, why," I asked myself, "can't I get started with this proof?"

Then another more helpful question occurred to me. "How did Euclid know to use the statements and reasons he used in his proof?" My eyes happened to fall on steps 4 and 5 instead of step 1, and, accidentally or unconsciously, I started to invert! I glanced back at the simple figure.

Perhaps he saw first that if he subtracted angle *COB* from angle *AOB* and angle *COB* from angle *COD*, the resulting angles *AOC* and *BOD* would be equal. And he could prove this if angle *AOB* was equal to angle *COD*. They were, because they were both straight lines, as given!

137

That might well have been the way Euclid went about his reasoning before he wrote down his neat little proof, I thought. That might be the reasoning *behind* his proof. I could scarcely wait to see if I could apply the same approach to a proof I was assigned:

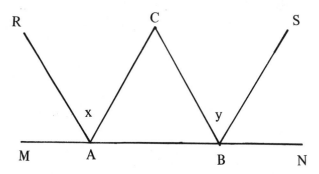

Given: Straight line *MN;* angle *CAB* equal to angle *CBA;* *AR* bisects angle *MAC; BS* bisects angle *NBC.*

Prove: Angle *x* equals angle *y.*

This time I didn't worry about starting with the "given" and reasoning down to the statement "angle *x* equals angle *y.*" I asked myself instead, "What relationships do I need in order to prove angle *x* equals angle *y?*"

I looked closely at the given, and sure enough, as I expected, it stated that *RA* bisected angle *MAC* and that *SB* bisected angle *NBC.* So I could use that. But it didn't state that angle *MAC* equalled angle *NBC.* "How can I prove that?" I pondered.

I looked back at the figure a moment and rubbed my forehead. "If angle *CAB* is equal to angle *CBA,* then I can prove that angle *MAC* equals angle *NBC* if *MN* is a straight line." I knew that the postulate "Supplements of equal angles are equal" had already been proved, and I could use it as a reason in my proof. It was given that *MN* was a straight line.

138

Euclid Inverted

So now all I, had to do was *invert* the order in which I had considered conditions, give reasons, and I'd have my *formal* proof. I'd found out how to get *my* viewpoint on the work, even if it involved first getting *behind* the formal proof. Now I could write my proof:

Statements	Reasons
1. *MN* is a straight line.	1. Given.
2. Angles *MAB* and *ABN* are straight angles.	2. Definition of a straight angle.
3. Angle *MAC* is a supplement of angle *BAC;* angle *NBC* is a supplement of angle *ABC.*	3. If the sum of two angles is a straight angle, they are supplements of each other.
4. Angle *CAB* equals angle *ČBA.*	4. Given.
5. Angle *MAC* equals angle *NBC.*	5. Supplements of equal angles are equal.
6. *RA* bisects angle *MAC,* and *SB* bisects angle *NBC.*	6. Given.
7. Angle *x* is equal to one-half of angle *MAC;* angle *y* is equal to one-half of angle *NBC.*	7. Bisectors of angles divide them into equal halves.
8. Therefore angle *x* equals angle *y.*	8. Step 5, and halves of equals are equal!

I learned later in the textbook that the way I reasoned before I wrote the formal proof was called *indirect reasoning;* that is, from what was to be proved I was leading to the given conditions. The formal proof was called *deductive reasoning,* leading *from* the given to the conclusion desired.

Deductive proofs in the text reminded me of tinkertoys. You

139

could build all sorts of strange shapes if you just started snapping parts together with no apparent plan. Of course, there was a plan, but I couldn't see it. What I had to do was jump over to the conclusion so I could deduce the steps that got me there. That was like sorting out the parts of a tinkertoy set so I could build the toy I wanted, it seemed to me.

Finally I realized that if I wanted to prove what I was assigned to prove, first I needed to get a viewpoint from the "prove" end and look back toward the given, just the *inverse* of starting with the given and trying to look toward the "prove." The "given" made a much bigger target for indirect reasoning than the "prove" did for deductive reasoning. Once I had done the indirect reasoning, it was easy to *invert* and write it down in the formal, deductive manner.

Just as I'd preferred to have a goal in mind when I'd started snapping tinkertoy parts together, I liked first to work from the viewpoint of what was to be proved. Let's say I wanted to prove statement A. First I'd think what I needed to prove A, say statements B and C. Then I'd look again at the given to see if I had B and C. Suppose B was given but C wasn't. Then I'd ask myself what I needed to prove C. Let's call what I needed D and E. Then I'd look at the given and the figure to see if I could arrive at D and E. If so, then after doing the indirect reasoning, all I had to do was invert it and write down the deductive or formal proof, including reasons to justify the statements.

The indirect reasoning, the reasoning behind the deductive reasoning and formal proof, is precisely the kind of reasoning that lets *you* into the act when you are doing the problem. Indirect or inductive reasoning, as it is sometimes called, makes possible the introduction of the questioning, personal viewpoint necessary for any real understanding.

Inductive or indirect reasoning is the systematic way of deciding on the steps (in reverse order) for formal, deductive proof. Inductive reasoning is personal and questioning; deductive proof is impersonal and answering. They are really two sides of the same coin, and you have to know both sides to have an effective understanding of either one.

After I made the breakthrough of learning to take my viewpoint from what was to be proved and then to look at the given, I didn't have much trouble with geometry. I'd learned to invert deductive proofs given in the text so that I could see *how* they were probably worked out inductively by asking questions in the first place. Seeing *how* now seemed as important as seeing *what* was put down in deductive form. The *how* part involved seeing behind Euclid. In working proofs I was assigned, I invariably thought them through inductively before writing them down deductively.

Soon after my discovery, I began to realize something else that proved important to me. That was the need not only to understand the definitions, axioms, postulates, theorems, and corollaries, but also to get them thoroughly memorized. I found that the better I had them memorized the more quickly I could understand new theorems and work out new proofs.

To help me memorize the axioms, postulates, and so on, I wrote them down in order on four-by-six-inch cards. On one side I wrote what each was about, and on the reverse side I made any drawings necessary, along with a proof if one was involved. Every day or two I would flip through them, a kind of inversion from words to drawings in some cases, or *vice versa*. I'd barely glance at a postulate, for example, and then I'd try to recall it exactly as I had it drawn and written out.

I know that some teachers tell students not to memorize. But I found that memorizing not only helped me to select the axioms and so on that I needed for my proofs, but also saved me time from worrying whether I had my reasons in the proof worded accurately.

Before I started studying geometry, though, I'd already accepted the importance of both inversion and repetition. In geometry my main problem was to recognize the need for inversion and the kind of inversion involved. The principle rules

I learned for myself in my early experience with geometry might be expressed like this:

1) If you want to understand a given mathematical proof,
    a) follow it through step by step, reading it aloud and copying it down if you have trouble understanding it;
    b) invert the steps and, looking at the last one, ask yourself what you need to prove it;
    c) then reason step by step back to the first steps, back to the given.
2) If you are to give a formal or deductive proof of a relationship from given conditions,
    a) start from the "prove," asking yourself what you need to justify the relationship;
    b) reason step by step back to the given relationships;
    c) now invert the order of the steps, write them down, and you have the formal, deductive proof.

If you want to try to convince someone how smart you are, do as Euclid did and show him only the formal, deductive part of your work. But if you want to teach him, do as Descartes did and show him both your method—the inductive or indirect part of your work—and the deductive part. That course, I think, is by far the nobler one.

142

CHAPTER 12

CONVERSION AND INVERSION:
Word Problems in Math and Science

If you are like 90 percent of students, you'd much rather solve a complicated equation than set up and solve a simple math problem stated in words. But if you've read the two previous chapters with reasonable care and have practiced their principles, you're just about converted from the 90 percent to the 10 percent who'd rather solve a word problem.

Actually, your ability to do word problems is as important in understanding science and engineering as your ability to solve equations. You have to know how to do both, but if you can set up their equations, most word problems are more than half solved.

In this chapter you'll learn to apply the principle of inversion to word problems. You'll also discover that when you get stuck with a problem, the best way to get unstuck is by making up a similar problem. You'll find, too, that you can use the same inversion approach to statement problems in both math and the sciences.

Working a statement problem is a little like eating a pie. If you try to take it in all at once, you'll choke. If you divide it into parts you can handle, you can enjoy it. Maybe it's too much to hope that you'll be as eager to try a word problem after looking at it as you would be to eat a pie you see when you're hungry. But remember that in both cases, you've got to cut the whole into parts. You do so with problems by asking many simple questions.

If you start asking questions about the right part of the problem and ask enough simple questions, you're fairly certain to find the solution. The procedure is similar to that of doing proofs in geometry.

Once it's done, it looks simple. A huge sign once hung in a General Motors research laboratory: "This problem will be simple when solved." It might have added, "This problem will be solved when enough simple answers are found to simple questions about the problem." Before you can find an answer, you must have a question.

So after reading through a problem, you want to start taking it apart by asking the question, "What is the problem calling for?" Often you are not told this until the end of the problem. Just as in doing a geometrical proof, you invert and start with what is to be found and reason back to the data of the problem, asking simple questions and finding simple answers each step of the way.

Of course, you need to represent "what is to be found" with some letter value. If you had a number for it, you wouldn't have a problem.

Let's take as an example a typical algebra problem: "Thirty-six coins consisting of nickels and dimes amount to $2.25. Find the number of nickels and dimes."

First, we must ask the question that opens the door of any word problem and gives us a point of view: "What is the problem calling for?" The answer is the number of nickels and the number of dimes.

So we have two unknowns, which we have to translate into the language of algebra. The next question, then, is "What letter shall we let represent the number of nickels?" X, let's say. So we write, "Let x=the number of nickels."

The next question we have to ask is, "What relationship does the number of nickels have to the number of dimes?" Looking at the problem again, we notice that there are 36 coins altogether.

Suppose we can't decide how to relate the number of dimes and nickels. Rather than give up, let's use one of the most effective methods I've found of getting unstuck at this point in a problem. Let's pretend temporarily that we *have* a numerical value for x.

Let's suppose there are 10 nickels (10 is an easy number to subtract, add, multiply, or divide). If there were 10 nickels, how many dimes would you say there are? 26? Of course. How did you get it? You subtracted 10 from 36, you say. That is 36-10=26. (Notice the inversion of the order of 10 and 36.)

But we *don't* know there are 10 nickels. We decided to let x represent the number of nickels. So now instead of saying 36-10 equals the number of dimes, which we only supposed, we can say, 36-x= the number of dimes. Okay?

Now we have

> Let x= the number of nickels;
> 36-x= the number of dimes.

Where do we go from here? We need an equation to solve for x. It's time to look at the problem again. The coins are worth $2.25, it says. We've already used the fact that there are 36 coins.

If they were all dimes, how much would they be worth? $3.60. And if they were all nickels? $1.80. So there have to be some nickels and some dimes.

You probably see how to set up the equation already, but suppose that you just can't figure out what to do next. You scratch your head, squirm in your seat, grit your teeth, and maybe still nothing occurs to you.

Do you want to know what I did the first time I found myself in such a predicament? No, I didn't call someone and ask for an explanation or learn what to do in class the next day—although I might have done one or the other had they been possible. After much agitation and annoyance, finally I had an idea that I've used many times since, one that was much more enlightening to me than finding out how someone else did the problem.

I decided to make up a similar problem whose answers I'd know in advance. I invert the usual problem. Starting with the answers, I solve for the questions! So I know the problem backwards and forwards.

Suppose you and I were stuck with the problem we've been considering. Let's make up a similar problem where the number of nickels is 20 and the number of dimes is 30, making the total number of coins 50. The value of the dimes is $3.00, and the value of the nickels is $1.00. So the coins together are worth $4.00.

Wording our new problem like the original, we'd have, "Fifty coins consisting of nickels and dimes amount to $4.00. Find the number of nickels and dimes."

As we did before, we could let x equal the number of nickels. Then 50-x equals the number of dimes. But how do we decide that the value of the coins is $4.00? Of course, we take 5 times 20 and add the result to 10 times 30 for the value in cents. That is,

$$5(20)\text{cents} + 10(30)\text{cents} = 400 \text{ cents.}$$

Or, if we didn't know the number of nickels or dimes, we'd substitute in the letter value representing the number of nickels and the expression representing the number of dimes,

$$5(x) + 10(50\text{-}x) = 400;$$
$$5x + 500\text{-}10x = 400;$$

$$-5x = 400\text{-}500;$$
$$-5x = -100;$$
$$x = 20, \text{ the number of nickels;}$$
$$50\text{-}x = 50\text{-}20 = 30, \text{ the number of dimes.}$$

Since our answer checks with the problem we made up, it seems pretty certain that our method is correct. Let's apply it to our original problem. We had,

Let x = the number of nickels;
$36\text{-}x$ = the number of dimes.

Now, the value of the nickels plus the value of the dimes is equal to $2.25, which is 225 cents, of course.

$$5x + 10 (36 - x) = 225;$$
$$5x + 360 - 10x = 225$$
$$-5x = 225\text{-}360 = -135$$
$$x = \frac{-135}{-5} = 27, \text{ the number of nickels;}$$

$36\text{-}x = 36\text{-}27 = 9$, the number of dimes.

Let's check,
$$5(27) + 10(9) = 225;$$
$$135 + 90 = 225;$$
$$225 = 225.$$

It's pretty simple, isn't it? Perhaps you're tempted to ask "Why go to so much trouble thinking about a problem tha turns out to be so simple? Why not just tell me this and this anc this and you have the answer?"

Why not? Because I want *you* to develop an approach to solving word problems that can apply to all word problems. Maybe you're already thinking that there's an easier way to do the problem, perhaps by using two letters for the two unknowns?

Okay, let's try to do the problem with two letters for the unknowns. The beginning is the same. We start by asking what the problem calls for. As before, we write first, "Let x = the number of nickels."

Now, instead of worrying about the relationship between the number of nickels and dimes, we can go ahead and write, "Let y = the number of dimes."

Having already reasoned through an equation, we can now write, "$5(x) + 10(y) = 225$."

But regardless how much we try to solve a single equation with two unknowns, we can't do it. Let's see if we can get another equation. What do x and y represent? The number of nickels and the number of dimes, of course. So if we add them, we get the total number of coins. Right?

$$x + y = 36;$$
$$y = 36\text{-}x = \text{the number of dimes.}$$

And we're back where we started as soon as we substitute 36-x for y in the first equation of both unknowns,

$$5(x) + 10(36\text{-}x) = 225;$$
$$5x + 360\text{-}10x = 225;$$
$$-5x = 225\text{-}360 = -135;$$
$$x = 27, \text{ the number of nickels;}$$
$$36\text{-}x = 36\text{-}27 = 9, \text{ the number of dimes.}$$

Or we could have solved the equations simultaneously,

$$x + y = 36;$$
$$5x + 10y = 225.$$

Multiplying every term by -10 in the first equation above, we have,

$$-10x\text{-}10y = -360;$$
$$5x + 10y = 225$$

-5*x* + 0 = -135, adding the two equations;
x = 27, the number of nickels;
27 + *y* = 36;
y = 9, the number of dimes.

So, you see there are at least three ways of arriving at the solution. But the important things to remember are these: We started each method by asking what the problem calls for; then we considered the data; and in each case if we had gotten stuck, we could have gotten unstuck by making up a similar problem to see how to use the letter values. That is, we could have inverted and used an *If we were making up the problem* approach.

Of course, there are many types of statement problems in math and science. You have to learn new concepts and definitions, and you may have to study example problems. But you don't have to make the mistake that many students make. You don't have to memorize every type of word problem you are able to solve.

You can make the principle of inversion and inductive reasoning a way of approaching all word problems, whether they are in math or in the sciences. To help fix the principle in your mind, let's consider a couple more algebra problems and a physics problem.

A Mixture Problem: "How many quarts of 80 percent alcohol must be added to 6 quarts of 50 percent alcohol to produce a 60 percent mixture?"

Do you remember your usual first question for a word problem? It's, "What is the problem calling for?" What this problem calls for is at the beginning of the problem. There is only one unknown, the number of quarts of 80 percent alcohol to be added. So we write, "Let *x* = the number of quarts of 80 percent alcohol to be added."

Many students find a sketch helpful in solving mixture

problems. It is a matter of translating words into pictures. We can imagine a container for the unknown number of quarts of 80 percent alcohol, another for the 6 quarts of 50 percent alcohol, and a third containing the mixture after the contents of the first two are added.

x quarts   +   6 quarts   =   (x + 6) quarts

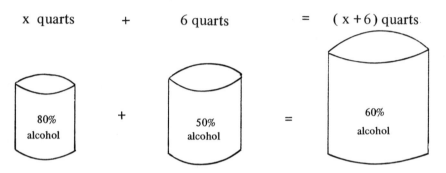

To help us see the relations even a little better, let's imagine that the alcohol has settled to the bottom of each container (even though the reverse is more likely!).

x quarts   +   6 quarts   =   (x + 6) quarts

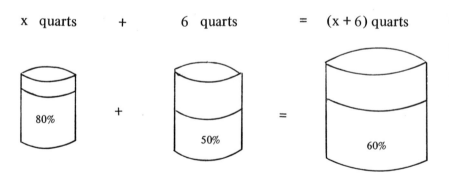

How are the amounts of alcohol in the first two cans related to the amount in the right-hand can after the contents of the first two cans are poured into it? They're equal, aren't they? So we have the equation,

150

$$80\% \; x + 50\% \;(6) = 60\% \;(x+6);$$

$$\frac{8\cancel{0}}{10\cancel{0}}x + \frac{5\cancel{0}}{10\cancel{0}}\,6 = \frac{6\cancel{0}}{10\cancel{0}}(x+6);$$

$$8x + 30 = 6x + 36;$$

$$8x - 6x = 36 - 30;$$

$$2x = 6;$$

$$x = \frac{6}{2} = 3.$$

The answer to the problem is 3 quarts. Wasn't that easy when we visualized the problem? Let's try another.

A Distance Problem: "A jet plane can go 400 miles more per hour than twice the speed of a passenger train. If the train can go 330 miles in the same time the plane can fly 2,420 miles, find the rate of each."

What does the problem call for? Here we have two unknowns, the speed of the train and the speed of the plane. First, we can write, "Let x = speed of train (number of miles per hour)."

But what about the speed of the plane? We look at the problem. The speed of the plane is more than twice the speed of the passenger train. So the speed of the plane is $2x$ plus what? Plus 400, of course. We can write, then, "Let $2x + 400$ = speed of the plane."

What three quantities are involved in this distance and rate problem? Rate in miles per hour, time in hours, and distance in miles. If you are like many students, you'll find a little chart helpful in solving this type of problem. Always enter the data containing the letter value first.

151

	Distance	Rate	Time
Train		x	
Plane		2x + 400	

Although you'll need to use only one chart, we'll repeat this one to make sure you see how to enter the data. After we enter the data containing the letter value, we look again at the problem for numerical facts. The train goes 330 miles; the plane goes 2,420. We enter these data in the distance column.

	Distance	Rate	Time
Train	330	x	
Plane	2420	2x + 400	

We don't need to look at the problem for our next entry. The last column filled in—whether it's the left, middle, or right—is filled in from data in the other two columns. But we must first ask ourselves what the relationship is between distance, rate, and time. If we travel 50 miles per hour and travel for 3 hours, how far do we go? Probably without hesitation you say 150 miles. How did you get it? You multiplied the rate times the time: 3 times 50.

Distance equals rate multiplied by time. If d represents distance; r, rate; and t, time, then $d = rt$.

How do we solve for t? As you remember, if t is multiplied by some value, and we wish to solve for t, we must divide,

$$\frac{d}{r} = \frac{rt}{r} \; ; \; t = \frac{d}{r} \; .$$

This means that to complete our chart, we divide the data in the distance column by the data in the rate column.

	Distance	Rate	Time
Train	330	x	$\dfrac{330}{x}$
Plane	2420	2x + 400	$\dfrac{2420}{2x+400}$

Now we have to find the relationship between the time for the train and the time for the plane, since the time column is the last one filled in for this problem. We look back at the problem and see that it states "same time." So we have an equation:

$$\frac{330}{x} = \frac{2420}{2x+400} = \frac{2(1210)}{2(x+200)} ;$$

$$\frac{330}{x} = \frac{1210}{x+200} ;$$

$$x(x+200)\frac{330}{x} = \frac{1210}{(x+200)}x(x+200),$$

multiplying both sides by the same value,

$$\frac{330(x+200)}{2} = \frac{1210x}{2} , \text{dividing both sides by 2;}$$

$$165(x+200) = 605x;$$

$$165x + 165(200) = 605x;$$

$$165x - 605x = -165(200);$$

$$-440x = -165(200);$$

$$x = \frac{\cancel{11}(15)(\cancel{200})^{5}}{\cancel{11}(\cancel{40})} = 75.$$

We have the answers to the problem, then: The speed of the train is 75 miles per hour, and the speed of the plane is 550 miles per hour. As you may have noticed, factoring numbers often eliminates a lot of work.

Problems in textbooks are nearly always artificial. In real science and engineering situations, you often have to spell out your problem and find your data in handbooks or go to the laboratory and set up experiments to determine the data you need.

Most engineers, though, can find all the data they need from handbooks and other publications on experiments already performed. In designing a bridge, for example, they have to decide how wide it is to be, the kinds of materials to be used, and the distance it is to span—just as a start. In a sense, they have to make up their problems and find much of their data for the solutions from shelves of reference books.

But long before they reach this point, engineering students must learn to solve problems someone else makes up. As we have seen, making up a problem is just the inverse of solving one someone else has composed.

Fortunately, the same principles of inversion that apply to algebra word problems also apply to problems in engineering, physics, and chemistry textbooks. Let me show you what I mean by considering a rather typical physics problem.

Inversion in a Physics Problem: "A train of mass 500 tons starts from rest and covers 1000 feet in one minute. Assuming a uniform acceleration, what is the force exerted by the locomotive?"

We start with the usual first question: What is the problem calling for? The answer is at the end of the problem: the force exerted by the locomotive.

To solve the problem, you almost have to be familiar enough with physics for the formula $F=ma$ to suggest itself to you. F stands for force, m for mass, and a for acceleration. So we can solve the problem if we know the mass and acceleration involved.

The mass is 500 tons, which we'll need to convert to pounds, since the normal units in the English system are feet for distance, pounds for mass, seconds for time, and foot poundals (foot pound/sec^2) for force. One ton is equal to 2000 pounds. From this relationship we can write two conversion ratios:

$$\frac{2000 \text{ pounds}}{1 \text{ ton}} = \frac{1 \text{ ton}}{2000 \text{ pounds}} = 1$$

To convert tons to pounds, we multiply by one of these ratios. Going back to the fraction-ratio principle, we can think of 500 as being multiplied by "tons"; so we need the ratio that has tons in the diviser; that is, in the denominator:

$$500 \text{ tons} = 500 \text{ tons} \cdot \frac{2000 \text{ pounds}}{1 \text{ ton}}$$

$$= 1{,}000{,}000 \text{ pounds}$$

Now we have the mass in the units we need, but our problem doesn't give acceleration as such. What is the acceleration? It is how fast the speed of an object is changing, and the unit we want it in is feet/sec^2. Three acceleration formulas should be thoroughly memorized by physics students and should suggest themselves to them at this point, both as a letter formula and in words:

1) $v_f = v_o + at$ (Final velocity equals beginning velocity plus acceleration times the time.)

2) $v_f^2 = v_o^2 + 2as$ (The square of the final velocity equals the square of the initial velocity plus twice the acceleration times the distance.)

3) $s = v_0 t + \frac{1}{2}at^2$ (Distance equals the initial velocity times the time plus one-half the acceleration times the square of the time.)

The question now is, "How do we decide which of the three acceleration formulas we need to use?" Let's look again at the problem and see which of the factors for the equations we have given. We find that the distance the locomotive travels is 1000 feet. The time is 1 minute or 60 seconds. Since the locomotive starts from rest, we know the initial velocity is zero.

We glance at the three formulas that we have jotted down. The first contains two values that we don't have given, the final velocity and the acceleration. We need a formula with only one unknown, if we can find it. So we look at the second equation. It also has two unknowns, final velocity and acceleration. We turn to the third. (With practice, you can do this in less time than it takes to tell about it.) The third equation contains only one value that we don't have given. So it is the equation we want to use:

$$s = v_0 t + \frac{1}{2}at^2 ;$$

$$1000 \text{ feet} = 0 \frac{ft}{sec^2} \cdot 60 \text{ sec} + \frac{1}{2} a (60 \text{ sec})^2 ;$$

$$1000 \text{ ft.} = 0 + \frac{1}{2} a \ 3600 \text{ sec}^2 ;$$

$$1000 \text{ ft.} = a \cdot 1800 \text{ sec}^2 ;$$

$$\frac{1000 \text{ ft}}{1800 \text{ sec}^2} = a , \quad \text{dividing both sides by same value.}$$

$$a = \frac{5}{9} \frac{ft}{sec^2}.$$

Now we can use the formula that first occurred to us, *F=ma*, and soon we have our solution,

$$F = ma;$$

$$F = 1,000,000 \text{ pounds} \cdot \frac{5}{9} \frac{ft}{sec^2}$$

$$= 555,556 \text{ ft. poundals;}$$

or 556,000 ft poundals to nearest 1,000.

So you see that a problem is pretty easy if we have a way of getting into it, if we divide it into parts we can handle, and if we are familiar with the basic formulas of the science.

Students who solve such a problem without memorizing a problem type are often inclined to invert the steps and conceal their method when they present their solution. And some teachers are also inclined to present their solution in a deductive manner that gives students little idea how to solve a problem for themselves. A deductive solution to the problem above would go much line this:

Given: mass = 500 tons; distance = 1000 ft.; time = 60 sec.

$$s = v_0 t + \tfrac{1}{2} a t^2;$$

$$1000 \text{ ft.} = 0 + \tfrac{1}{2} a (60 \text{ sec})^2;$$

$$1000 \text{ ft.} = \frac{1}{2} 3600 \text{ sec}^2 a;$$

$$a = \frac{1000 \text{ ft}}{1800 \text{ sec}^2} = \frac{5}{9} \frac{ft}{sec^2};$$

$$F = ma;$$

$$= 1,000,000 \text{ pounds} \cdot \frac{5}{9} \frac{ft}{sec^2};$$

$$= 555,556 \text{ ft. poundals}.$$

It's a nice, neat solution. But if you didn't understand the reasoning behind it, you might not learn much from watching it performed.

With only slight modification, the summary of what I learned about mathematical proof can serve as a summary of the main points of this chapter.

1) If you want to understand an example problem given in the usual deductive manner,
    a) first, follow it through step by step, reading it aloud and copying it down if you have any trouble understanding it;
    b) second, invert the steps and, looking at the last one, ask yourself what data was needed for it;
    c) then reason in the same way step by step back to the first steps.
2) If you are to solve a word problem,
    a) start from "what is to be found," asking yourself what you need—formulas, etc.—to find it;
    b) using what formulas you need, work back to the given conditions;
    c) if you get stuck, make up a similar problem;
    d) if you are to give a "formal," deductive solution, reverse the steps of your indirect or inductive solution.

It may be that from simply reading the last three chapters, you are not yet converted from the 90 percent of students who would rather do a complicated equation than a word problem. But I am confident that when you put the principles of this chapter into practice a few times, you will begin to prefer word problems.

You will have cleared away much of the confusion and uncertainty that often plagues students of trigonometry and calculus. You will have gone a long way toward a good understanding of how engineers and scientists think about problems. And you will have a better grasp of the kind of thinking that produced the age of science and technology we live in.

CHAPTER 13

THE DOUBLE TAKE:
The Art of Taking Lecture Notes

Imagine, if you can, that you are a professor lecturing to a class of freshmen and sophomores.

Even though it's a ten-o'clock class, a couple of knuckleheads have already fallen asleep in the back row before the period is half over. A blonde with soulful blue eyes stares out the window. A football player a couple of seats away ogles her. Neither is paying attention to the gems of wisdom you've collected and culled and polished over the years.

You catch the eyes of some students in the third row who seem to be listening. About half of them are writing a line or two in notebooks now and then. Most of the rest are just listening. But a couple of students glance up occasionally, seem to reflect a moment, and then resume quickly their almost constant note taking. Once or twice during each lecture, they raise their hands to ask for clarification of some point or to restate an idea in their own words to see if they've understood it.

Now imagine that a couple of months later you have the task most teachers hate most. You're deciding on the grades your students are to receive for the semester's work. When you're trying to decide between giving a student an *A* or *B*, a *B* or *C*, a *C* or *D*, you can't help but react to the sum of your impressions of the student as he responded to your lectures.

You have no problem with a few of the students who asked good questions and kept busy taking good notes. They have the strongest *A*'s, anyway. But in those border-line cases, you just can't keep out your impressions of the students. And you can't eliminate the feeling that those students who seemed to be taking good notes are more interested in learning and deserve the better grade when the test scores leave you in doubt.

The test scores of the blonde with the soulful blue eyes are almost as good as those of a not-so-pretty brunette who seemed to keep busy taking notes. But reluctantly you give the blonde a *C+* and the brunette a *B-*. One sharp so-and-so has the maximum number of class cuts allowed by the college, yet he has still managed to make slightly better test scores than another good student who has no absences and who has appeared to take good notes. Nevertheless, you give the sharp so-and-so a *B+* and the other student an *A-*.

Are you tired of imagining yourself as a professor? Well, you've imagined yourself as one long enough to see one important reason for taking good notes—if you like good grades. When the chips are down, the impression you leave on a teacher while you take good notes day after day may make the difference between one letter grade and the next lower one.

But even though it may be the most dramatic reason, this matter of making a good psychological impression on the teacher is only one of several reasons for taking good notes. It can create a good psychological impression on you, too. It keeps you alert in class. It makes attendance at the lecture an active process. It makes remembering the lecture easier, because it combines the passive process of hearing the professor's ideas with the active process of deciding on and writing down the most important ones so that you can see them. And it gives you a permanent record of the points your teacher stresses.

While you are busy listening and taking notes—and these processes must take place at the same time—you will feel that you're spending the lecture hour in the best way you can. And for good reason. When you're busy taking notes, you *are* making the most of your time in class.

Many students I've tutored have complained of having trouble concentrating, or even staying awake, in some lecture classes—until they learned to stay busy taking notes. It's hard to go to sleep while you're writing. And if you're concentrating enough on what your professor is saying to find statements to write down, you won't start woolgathering in daydreams about your next party or the next football game.

With the concentration necessary for good note-taking, you make it easier to learn the material of a course. The teacher provides an aspect of learning you may not get any other way: the aural or hearing aspect. "Faith cometh by hearing." And much knowledge also comes by hearing. Concentrating on hearing your teacher's words and writing some of those words down, you are much more likely to remember what your teacher says.

Even though you may consider that much or most of what your teacher says is unimportant, you have the assurance that you haven't missed any important points of his lectures if you listen attentively and take many notes. Also, teachers often give hints of what you can expect on examinations. If you make notes of these hints, you're more likely to be prepared for exams than the students who are lax in their note-taking habits.

Taking good notes also helps give the confidence that comes from feeling that you're learning what your teacher expects you to learn from a course. If you know well what a teacher emphasizes in his lectures, you may do fairly well on examinations even if you don't get to do all the assigned reading. One of my students, who had the equivalent of a fair tenth-grade education when he started to college, managed to graduate with a *C+* average—mainly on the strength of excellent notes, regular class attendance, and frequent participation in class discussions. He tried all sorts of ways to increase his reading speed, but his defective vision at close range kept him a slow reader. Learning to take good notes was the difference between graduation and failure for this former student of mine, now an executive in an oil company.

Class time not spent taking notes seems to me to be time half wasted. You're supposed to attend class; so you might as well put class time to the best possible use. That involves, first, the desire to take good notes and, second, the development of good note-taking techniques.

When I was finishing high school and hoping to go to college, I took shorthand to help prepare me to take lecture notes. I had the idea that you ought to write down everything a professor says, if possible.

During my first straight-lecture course, a class in American history, I decided that complete, verbatim notes were not necessary. For the first four or five weeks, I took about half my notes in shorthand, and every two or three days I would copy them, transcribing the shorthand into longhand. About the fifth week, I got sick and missed three or four lectures; so almost two weeks passed before I got around to trying to transcribe my last few days of lecture notes. Alas, my shorthand was too cold and too imperfect. I just about decided to give up taking notes in shorthand.

After returning to class, I tried taking all my notes in longhand and found that I could take them at the rate of over twenty words a minute, or over one thousand words (five or six notebook pages) in a fifty-minute lecture. I decided that I could surely get down the main points of a lecture in that many words. I felt that transcribing shorthand notes was not the best way to spend my time. I found, too, that taking notes in longhand was good practice in the kind of discrimination I had to use in taking quizzes, when I couldn't write down everything I knew but had to decide what was most important.

The experience of a student who went through my college four or five years later confirmed my discovery. A former navy stenographer responsible for taking down verbatim the words of a ship's captain and transcribing them into typed copy, this student decided to take his college notes the same way. He took down every word his teachers said in class each day. Then at night he typed his shorthand notes and placed his typed copy in a binder. Each time he reviewed his notes he had six or eight times as much to study as students who took notes at the rate I did. He wasn't practicing discrimination. He treated everything a teacher said as if it were equally important. Although he was a good *B* student, I think he might have been a better one if he had not taken such complete notes or spent so much time typing them.

My brief experience with attempting to take part of my notes in shorthand taught me one thing, however. I could take enough notes in longhand—provided I kept busy writing—even if it meant writing down some things not very important. My first rule for taking notes, then, was *keep writing.*

In my note taking, I soon discovered that I tended not to start writing again if I paused very long after catching up on what I felt was important. Sometimes I would stop writing while a professor was telling a corny joke. (I always tried to take down the good ones!) After he was back on the subject of his lecture, I would suddenly discover that I'd missed a couple of points that I wished I'd written down. It didn't take many such experiences for me to learn this lesson: Even if a teacher's joke is corny, go ahead and summarize it. "Keep writing," I told myself.

At first I let this rule apply only when the teacher was talking. I didn't bother to make notes of students' questions if I thought they were unimportant. But here, too, I learned that if

I stopped taking notes, I had a tendency not to begin again until after I'd missed some important points. Before long I concluded that the only way I could take my best notes was to *keep writing,* even if it meant summarizing a student's unimportant question.

Of course, you're not very likely to take your best lecture notes your first semester, even if you practice the keep-writing rule. But if you learn to keep writing, your notes are sure to improve with practice.

Notes should always be taken in ink. The only time I ever took notes in pencil was when I got careless and ran out of ink. Pencil notes smear and are about twice as hard to read. So to save yourself some frustration, *take notes in ink.*

Far too often I've seen students' notebooks that contained notes for three or four courses. When students with such notes review for a quiz, they waste time trying to get all their notes together, and often they don't find them all. So be sure to *keep separate notebooks for each course.*

My own preference is for spiral-bound, 8½-by-11-inch, wide-line notebooks. After my first couple of semesters in college, I decided to bind separately the notebooks for each course. When I did so, I found that I'd not allowed enough room on the right-hand margins of my pages. As a result, it's harder to read those bound notes than it should be. Here is another rule, then: *Keep your writing at least one-half inch from the holes in your notebook.*

Before I took my first lecture course, I had read somewhere a suggestion about using hanging indentation for notes. I tried it and liked it so well that I used it for all my lecture notes in college. For hanging indentation, you start a paragraph at the left hand margin and indent the subsequent lines of the paragraph. When you start a new paragraph, go back to the left-hand margin. Main ideas seem to stand out more emphatically this way, possibly because hanging indentation is the inverse of the usual way of paragraphing. So for another suggestion, *try hanging indentation.*

Notes are not useful unless they are legible. If you are like a lot of students, you tend to let your penmanship get sloppy. To keep my notes legible and halfway pleasant to read, I found it useful to practice now and then (outside of class) the penmanship exercises I learned in grade school. If you have any trouble reading your notes, or if you would like to make them still more readable, *practice your penmanship.*

To be of any use notes not only have to be legible, but they also have to make sense. I have seen many outline notes that made no sense to the students who took them. The only kind of notes I've seen that are really understandable are complete-sentence notes. An important rule, then, is to *write your notes in complete sentences.*

Not long ago, I saw suggestions that students begin important ideas on the left-hand margin and indent sentences containing less important ideas. This is a variation of hanging indentation. The suggestion is fine, but don't worry too much about getting the important ideas over at the margin as you are taking notes. If you can do so, fine. When you review, though, you may find that you've indented an important idea. If so, you can underline it. You can make some decisions about the relative importance of sentences in your notes as you take them; you can make other decisions as you review.

Of course, you can't and shouldn't take down in longhand everything a professor says. At first you're likely to miss an important point now and then and get down some insignificant information. But with practice, you'll get down most of the important ideas. My notes were mainly in the phrases the teacher used. Often I began a sentence with a phrase the professor used at the beginning of one statement and concluded my sentence with a phrase from the end of another of the professor's statements.

Frequently an experienced teacher repeats important ideas in slightly different words and illustrates a general statement with a number of specific details. Often you'll have to leave out words and summarize your teacher's statements in your own words. You can learn to do this effectively if you'll follow the rule we've mentioned before—one that bears repetition—*keep writing.*

You should do most of your writing without abbreviations. An abbreviation is worthless if it cannot be understood quickly a month or year after you write it. Easily recognized, standard abbreviations, such as "U.S." or "etc.," are, of course, all right.

As you're taking notes, you may find you can't spell a word that you want to write. If that happens to you, spell it the best you can and leave space to correct it once you find the spelling in a dictionary or thesaurus.

By all means, date your notes at the beginning of each lecture. You may need to have your notes dated to know which ones to concentrate on for a particular test. I liked to include the lecture number too. For example, my notes for one of my history lectures begin, "December 7, Lecture 33."

If for some reason you have to miss a lecture, leave spaces in your notebook the next time you start taking notes, and try to borrow notes from a student in your class. Unless you're able to find someone who takes good notes, too, you will learn not to miss lectures! One student told me of his experience borrowing notes. His classmate's notes for the day included about a dozen phrases—along with doodles of two racing cars and three jet planes. You can imagine how much the classmate was learning from the lecture! *Notebooks are not for doodling.*

If you want to make the best use of class time, take neat, businesslike, full-sentence notes. You will improve your learning processes as you take them, and you will get notes that you can reread quickly during your study time the same day or later. In the process, you will be preparing an excellent springboard for your study for quizzes.

Of course, you will get better notes under some teachers than under others. Some teachers are just better than others.

The Double Take

You'll find it harder to take notes in classes with a great deal of discussion than under teachers who give well-organized lectures with few interruptions. The best solution to the problem of taking notes in a class where there are many interruptions is to try to get the best and most complete notes you can, even if it means writing down unimportant questions that some students ask.

You may find it more difficult to take notes in math or science classes where the teachers work problems or make drawings on the blackboard. If this happens, try using the left half of your note page for the problem or drawing and the right half to write down any of your teacher's comments you want to note.

As an example of some fairly good notes, I am going to give you part of my first day's notes in a survey course in European history. I chose the first day's notes to show how important it can be to take good notes the very first day. My professor told what the course was about and gave a way of dividing ideas and movements into five categories to make them easier to remember. Notice that my notes are in complete sentences, exactly as I worded them when I was a sophomore in college.

History 9
Lecture 1, Sept. 19

The period from the Renaissance to Waterloo is the most important period in history. During this period the end of the Middle Ages occurred through slow evolutionary changes. The main ideas of belief, of thinking, and of social values of present-day western civilization evolved during this period.

Five main categories or topics into which all the material of the course fit are 1) *political changes,* 2) *social changes,* 3) *economic changes,* 4) *intellectual changes,* 5) *religious changes.* Often they interact and intertwine.

1) The change from the Middle Ages to Modern (Early)

was very slow. The main feature of this political change was the breakup or dissolution of the feudal system. In its place arose the national state. Feudalism was a system of private govt.: those who had certain advantages controlled weaker peoples. The national state is a system of public law.

. . . .

5) The main change of intellectual character was from the medieval philosophy of blind faith to reason (in some cases to blind reason). In Middle Ages all philosophy was dogmatic. You took it from on high, read it from accepted books, and that was that. Age of reason replaced this period.

These five major topics are the crux of the course and involve the main problems of today. Of these the rise of the nation state is probably the most influential: Nationalism has with most become stronger than their religion.

REQUIREMENTS

Remember the outline above and tie things into it. You are required to be present 80% of the time. Class work consists of both lecture and recitation.

Discussion is encouraged.

Minimum requirement of outside reading is *900 pages.*

. . . .

All grades will be based on test results; also if it is on border line, attendance, class participation will help.

Wed. assign.

Introduction and Chapt. 1, Ergang.

These notes aren't bad, are they? They show that with practice and concentration you can take notes that don't have to be rewritten the same day in order to be of value. Written in blue-black ink, they are as legible and meaningful as they were immediately after the lecture.

168

The Double Take

You can learn to take notes that are as good or better than these by following the suggestions in this chapter. In summary, they are:

1) Use a separate notebook for each course, preferably an 8½-by-11-inch, spiral-bound, wide-line notebook.
2) Date each day's notes, and number the lecture.
3) Write in ink.
4) Try hanging indentation.
5) Write in complete sentences.
6) Abbreviate sparingly.
7) If you don't know how to spell a word, spell it the best you can and leave space for correction.
8) Leave at least a one-inch right-hand margin so your notes can be read easily in a binder.
9) Don't doodle in your notebook.
10) Keep busy writing.
11) Write in your teacher's jokes, too (it keeps you writing and makes your notes more interesting).
12) Practice your penmanship (good idea for both your notes and your exams).
13) Keep writing, and remember that your notes will improve with practice.

By taking good lecture notes, you often get a better idea of what to bear down on hardest in your study of the textbook and outside readings, a subject we'll go into in the next chapter.

By following the suggestions in this chapter, you'll get more out of your class attendance—even if some huge football lineman sits in front of you and keeps your professor from seeing whether you take notes or not. Listening with the concentration necessary for getting good notes, you take in aurally what the teacher has to say, and then you project the most important points onto your notebook, where you can take them in again visually. Thus you accomplish the double take, one of the best ways of impressing on your mind what you need to remember.

CHAPTER 14

THE DARKROOM OF THE MIND:
The Art and Craft of Study

Have you ever noticed a news photographer at a political or sporting event with three or four cameras dangling from his neck? Perhaps one of his cameras is set only for distant shots. Perhaps another is set for close-ups. One may be loaded with color film, others with black-and-white. The photographer may take dozens of shots during a news event. And from among them, only one or two may appear in the evening paper.

The reading that we discussed in an early chapter is much like this kind of photography. It is hurried, rapid, hopeful. Like the photographer who keeps clicking his shutters, hoping he will not miss an important gesture or scene, the rapid reader takes in phrase after phrase, idea after idea, trying to grasp the story or chapter or entire book as a whole. Just as the news photographer doesn't know which of the shots he will use, the rapid reader doesn't know which ideas he will utilize.

Study itself may be compared to the more careful, painstaking process of developing the film, selecting the best shots, cropping off the undesirable or unnecessary parts of a negative, and producing the finished enlargements to show to the editor.

Most of a student's time must be spent in a similar kind of effort. Practically all the study of a beginning language course or of mathematics or the sciences must be made up of this kind of work. Perhaps that is why students who come to college having already made a good record in math or in a foreign language rarely complain, "I just don't know how to study."

The photographer in a darkroom must follow several procedures that are somewhat like those of a student. He has to fix the film in a solution to keep the image from fading. He has to select which negatives to keep. He has to classify his negatives and file them so that he can find them when he needs them. And he has to be able to project the negative—by a process of inversion—onto photo paper that reproduces the image, much as he saw it originally.

Like the scenic photographer, the student may find that he needs to return to the site of his source and recapture a scene. He must select, of course, what is important to remember. He must be able to fix it in his mind, much as the photographer fixes a captured image in film. He must be able to arrange and classify what he learns so that he can recall what he knows—at least for the purpose of quizzes.

We have already considered effective ways of fixing a foreign language in your mind and of solving math and science problems. In this chapter we are concerned with ways of studying for the so-called reading courses, such as history, government, or literature.

How can you develop the kind of orderly, systematic approach to study that the photographer must have for his darkroom work? When I was going to college, my practice was first to read rapidly through an assignment. Then I would go through it a second time, underlining sentences or phrases I considered particularly important. I reread portions of the text that seemed hazy or especially important. The night or morning before a quiz I would try to gather my thoughts about the material, read my notes, and read the sentences I had underlined in the textbook.

This approach isn't bad. But shortly after I began tutoring, students started asking me what I thought of a five-step approach that they learned about in a speed-reading course at the university. Naturally I had to find out something about the five-step approach. What I learned sounded quite reasonable to me; so I started telling students about it and suggesting that it might be worth a try.

Soon students began reporting back to me that they found the five-step method of study quite useful. It helped them keep their minds on their subjects, and it helped them fix the main ideas of the text meaningfully in their minds.

You may want to try this effective five-step approach, too—particularly if, as you study, your mind tends to wander back to your last date or forward to the next football game!

As far as I've been able to learn, the five-step approach, sometimes called the "Survey Q3R Method," was first presented in Francis P. Robinson's *Effective Study* (Harper & Brothers, New York, 1946). Since that time, the method has been taught in various orientation and study courses around the country.

This five-step method is simple to learn, simple to apply, and simple to remember. Assuming that the text has headings or subtopics, first you read just these headings or subtopics. This is the survey. Second, you turn each heading into a question. Third, you start at the beginning of the chapter, look at the first heading, recall your question, and read down to the next heading, searching for answers to your question. Fourth, you answer the question, perhaps underlining the main sentences that provide the answer, and repeat the process with each heading. Fifth, you start once again at the beginning of the

172

chapter, look at the heading, recall the question and the answer you gave. This is the review step. "Survey Q3R"—survey, question, read, recite, review.

Taking an old government text, I'll give you a better idea of how the method works. Unless you are a pre-law student, or unless you have a good method of study, this subject—the federal taxing power—might tend to put you to sleep. In the first step, you just glance over the headings:

1) The taxing clause of the Constitution
2) Restrictions on the taxing power:
    a) Purposes
    b) Uniformity of indirect taxes
    c) Other express restrictions
    d) Implied restrictions
3) Wide sweep of the taxing power
4) The taxing power and social reform
5) The problem of multiple taxation . . .

These aren't all the headings in the chapter, but they give you an idea of the need for some way of approaching what is rather dry material for most students. If your text doesn't have headings, you will find it helpful to make headings of your own for it.

In the second, or question, step, you invert each of the headings into a question. For example,

1) What is the taxing clause of the Constitution?
2) What are the restrictions on the taxing power?
    a) What are the purposes of the restrictions?
    b) How are the indirect taxes uniform?
    c) What are the other express restrictions?
    d) What are the implied restrictions on the taxing power?
3) What is meant by "wide sweep of the taxing power"?
4) How are taxing power and social reform related?
5) What is the problem of multiple taxation?

Now you have glanced through the headings and mentally

inverted them into questions, much as a camera inverts an image into its negative. In the third step, you start at the beginning of the chapter, glance at the first heading, recall your question, and read to find the answer.

As you've seen, the first heading we considered can be turned into the question, "What is the taxing clause of the Constitution?" The answer lies in the last sentence before the next heading in the text. If I were studying in the manner I am suggesting here, I would underline the sentence, perhaps in red: "Very appropriately, the long list of powers given to Congress in the eighth section of the first article of the Constitution starts off with the power 'to lay and collect taxes, duties, imposts, and excises.' "

We now consider our second question, "What are the restrictions on the taxing power?" We find the answer in the sentence, "To begin with, Congress is not free to lay and collect taxes for any purpose, but only (as the Constitution plainly says) 'to pay the debts and provide for the common defense and general welfare of the United States.' "

You can see the plan of attack. The fourth step, then, is to recite and perhaps underline the answer to the question you've derived from the heading. The third and fourth steps, reading and reciting, should be done for each heading in turn.

In the fifth step, you glance at each heading, recall your question, and try to remember and recite your answer without looking at the underlined sentences. If you fail to recall the answer to your satisfaction, put a pencil dot by the heading so that you will pay special attention to the answer before your next quiz. The fifth step is the review step.

The whole method is as simple, as one, two, three, four, five—survey, question, read, recite, review. "Survey Q3R." But it forces you to keep your attention on the subject, to find answers to questions.

The five-step method makes conscious the process that a student greatly interested in his subject goes through unconsciously. Almost as quickly as a camera clicks and the image is inverted and captured on a roll of film, ideas invert themselves into questions and the answers are found—at least the answers the text gives. The best students pause occasionally and reflect on reasons they have for disagreeing with the textbook answers.

If you have to study subjects that don't interest you at first, and this happens to most students, I think you'll find the five-step Survey Q3R method a big help. It's helpful partly because no one can tell you *exactly* how to apply it. Every student who reads a particular text will have the same headings—if he pays any attention to them—but *you* have to turn each into *your* own question and find the sentences that contain the answer.

Some of my students find that it is not enough simply to underline the answers to their questions. They like to keep a notebook in which they write the sentences answering the questions or, preferably, a rewording of them into their own words. Writing the answers in a notebook can be somewhat tiring and time consuming, but I think it is much better than merely trying to outline a chapter. And it does require a projection of the answers into visual forms of your own making.

Earlier in this chapter we mentioned the importance of organizing your knowledge. When I was studying American history back in high school, I found it useful to relate the events of history to the terms of the presidents. I tried to imagine what was going on at a particular time in history. I tried to guess what newspapers were reporting and what people were talking about. You might say I tried to project myself back in time and space to imagine the hopes and feelings, the failures and triumphs of the people.

For example, I related the coming of the railroad and the beginning of the cattle drives to Abilene, Kansas, with the administration of Andrew Johnson. I didn't merely tie in the coming of the railroad with the date 1867, the middle of

Johnson's term. I tried to imagine the response of the few dozen settlers to the arrival of the first train.

I thought about the excitement that both the children and the adults must have felt as they heard the first train chug into the station. Having seen a few cowboy movies, it was easy for me to imagine huge herds of Texas longhorns come bawling into the large pens at Abilene for shipment east to Kansas City and on to Chicago.

I tried to tie in these mental pictures and "sound recordings" of events to statements in the text about the impact of the coming of the railroad and the shipping of cattle on the opening of the West. You might say that mentally I videotaped my impressions and the textbook generalizations, and then filed them under "Johnson's Administration—1865-69" for future reference, such as the time of the next quiz. All this made history much more interesting, exciting, and easy for me to remember. If I couldn't remember an important idea by sound, chances were I could remember it from a mental picture.

When I took a course on post-Civil War history in college, I immediately relearned the names of the presidents beginning with Lincoln and the years each served. Then each date or event I encountered I filed away under the right president's administration.

I associated the Spanish-American War with McKinley's administration, for instance. The Battle of San Juan Hill was the best-known battle of that war. Theodore Roosevelt became famous as the leader of the charge up San Juan Hill. Partly as the result of that fame, he was elected governor of New York and then vice-president and president of the United States. Once you develop a way to file the facts of history in your mind, you will soon have a clearer picture of causes and effects of events and how they relate to each other.

Some modern educators do not favor sheer memorization of names and dates; but as you see, you can make learning the names of presidents and the dates of their administrations more than mere memorization. You can make it a kind of mental file cabinet for your historical facts and impressions.

Modern educators have perhaps ridiculed too much what they call "rote memory." I am grateful for what little memorizing of poems and the like that I had to do. In memorizing, I was forced to see the way ideas or images tied together, and I had to develop my own schemes for remembering them. If a dozen of us were assigned the same poem to memorize, each of us learned and recited it a little differently, according to his own way of seeing the images and patterns and his own way of hearing the rhythms.

Some schemes for memorization that students figure out are so useful that they are passed on from class to class for decades. Every zoology and botany students needs to learn the Linnaean system of classifying plants and animals into "phyla, class, order, family, genus, and species" in that order. The order of classification can be learned in a minute by memorizing the simple statement, "Please come over for goodness sake," and then relating phyla to please, class to come, order to over, family to for, genus to goodness, and species to sake. Try it!

Organization is the key to successful school work. This is the way I suggest that you try to organize your work in reading courses:

1) Read, or at least scan the headings of, the entire text in the first week of the semester.
2) Read an assignment rapidly when it is assigned—before the teacher lectures on it.
3) Take good lecture notes.
4) Review your notes, and then *study* the textbook assignment:
    a) Survey—glance over the headings.
    b) Question—turn all the headings into questions.
    c) Read—read carefully for answers to the questions.
    d) Recite—say to yourself, underline, or write in a notebook your answers to the questions.

e) Review—starting at the beginning of the chapter, see if you can recall your answers to the questions, and put dots by headings that give you any trouble.

5) The night or morning before an exam, review notes and answers to headings in the text and your outside readings, discussing them with a classmate if you know one with whom you can work effectively.

In the next chapter, we will consider that ordeal that fills students with anxiety, fear, despair, and, for a fortunate few, the thrill of a challenge proudly accepted. We are speaking of that process by which teachers test the fruits of our efforts to learn—the exam.

As we said somewhere before, learning is largely a private matter. It takes place in the dark recesses of the mind. Our senses are the lenses that focus and invert impressions onto the film of our mind. But these impressions are of little use until they are developed, classified, and associated with previous memories, and until we are able to generate the inward light necessary to project them back through our voice, through the typed or written word, and through our actions.

To quote once again from Saint Francis of Assisi, "The only knowledge man has is what he can put to use." If you cannot recall and relate what you have learned, it is not yet knowledge. It is like a negative badly exposed or a good one that mistakenly winds up in the wastebasket of a photographer's darkroom.

If what you perceive is filed away where it can be recalled and projected and used, it is like a sharp photograph that may make you laugh or cry, fill you with anger or pity, cause you to double up a fist or to extend a helping hand. And it may even be just what you need to get a good grade on the next exam.

CHAPTER 15

TESTS—FROM TWO POINTS OF VIEW

Every college seems to have some version of the story about the professor who goes to the basement of his office building at midnight to grade his final examinations.

He doesn't go to the basement to escape the distraction of his family or the telephone. He goes at midnight because then there's no traffic up and down the stairs to hinder his mission.

Right at midnight he carefully opens his stuffed briefcase, takes out dozens of blue exam books, and starts tossing them toward the steps. When he runs out of exam books, he starts picking them up and entering grades in his little black book—according to how high they landed on the steps. And he has a weak arm!

Sometimes professors even tell this story on each other. But I've talked to enough teachers to know that, for most of them, making out tests is as troublesome to them as studying for exams is to their students. Grading tests, and particularly deciding on the final grades, can be as painful as taking the tests.

Teachers know, for instance, that the decision of whether to give a student a *B* or a *C*, a *C* or a *D,* may determine whether or not he gets into medical school. If the grade is on a border line, they have to try to estimate the effect of their bias for or against the student, the probability of his becoming a good or bad doctor, the fairness toward other students in giving him the better grade, the effect of tension on his test performance, the effect on the teacher's own sense of integrity. Deciding on a student's grade can be an agonizing task.

Teachers are aware that some students suffer more from "quiz nerves" than others. They know that nervous tension is a major factor in many students' failure to do as well as they might.

One physics teacher I know likes to tell the story of a student who decided he had the solution to his nervous tension when he first heard of the tranquilizer drugs. Wrangling a prescription somehow, Norbert felt he was fully prepared for his next physics test. He had studied hard, and about thirty minutes before the test, he took out his magic, little white tranquilizers. Just to play it safe, he thought, he doubled the dosage.

Norbert was very tranquil during the test. He looked calmly around at all the tense students near him. One was frowning and biting his lip as he stared at the problems. Another nervously dropped his slide rule. One was writing furiously, apparently afraid he'd forget a formula before he could write it down. Still another seemed to be staring into space, trying to conjure up a vision of a formula or an example problem.

But Norbert felt none of this tension and anxiety this time. He looked at the problems for a minute and was sure he could work them, but he didn't feel in the mood to start them just then. He stared directly at the test for a moment longer; then his mind wandered off toward more *tranquil* thoughts. In another month, the spring semester would be over. Smiling to himself, he thought of how much fun he would have on his summer job at a resort—and the hours off. That was the life—swimming, water skiing, and parties at the beach.

Suddenly, about ten minutes before the hour was over, Norbert came out of his reverie. His eyes focused again on the test before him, and he felt a momentary twinge of panic. Then he started tranquilly to work on the first of the five problems. But soon he realized there wasn't enough time to make a decent showing on the test. And he was even tranquil enough to go up to the professor and explain about the little white pills.

Fortunately, the teacher was understanding and felt the story was worth the effort of making out a new—and harder—test. So the teacher gained a new story, and Norbert got to make up the test. After one glance at the new test, he swore off tranquilizers for life.

The moral of the story is that for most students the value of a tranquilizer, or any other drug, is likely to be offset by its bad effects on his brain.

What is the solution, then, to the problem of too much tension at quiz time?

The solution, I think, is twofold. First, you need to learn a little about testing so that the prospect of a test won't be quite so fearsome. Second, you need to think about tests and the test situation as objectively and unemotionally as you can so that you can make nervous tension serve you rather than hinder you.

Deciding whether to give an objective test or an essay test is sometimes a big problem for a teacher. He has to spend a lot of time to make out a good objective test, but he can grade it rapidly. He can dash off several essay questions in a few minutes, but he has to spend a lot more time in grading an essay examination.

Knowing that some students do better on objective tests and others do better on essays, teachers often give one or two short essays and make the rest of the test objective. Or they may give an essay test one time and an objective test the next. If your teacher doesn't tell you what kind of quiz to prepare for, you'd better play it safe and prepare yourself for both types.

For an objective test, you may need to study more for minor details. But however well you study, you may find yourself having to guess on some questions. A knowledge of the motives of the average teacher can certainly help you to guess on the questions you're not quite sure of.

Professors take pride in trying to teach their students to see both sides of a question and to avoid extremes. So they tend to reward students who accept the word *generally* and who are cautious of the words *only, all, none,* and *always* on objective tests. For example, the statement, "Washington, D.C. is the *only* capital the United States has had," is false. So is the sentence, *"All* countries in Latin America touch on either the Atlantic or the Pacific Ocean."

Research studies of thousands of true-or-false statements from hundreds of teachers show, you should be glad to know, that:

1) Nine out of ten statements containing the word *only* were false.
2) Eight out of ten statements containing the word *none* were false.
3) Eight out of ten statements containing the word *all* were false.
4) More than seven out of ten statements containing the word *always* were false.
5) More than six out of ten *because* statements were false.
6) More than seven out of ten statements containing the word *generally* were true.
7) The longer a statement, the more likely it was to be true.

Knowing these probabilities is no substitute for knowing the material you're tested on. But if you must guess, these figures should improve your odds on guessing correctly.

Often the words *only, none, all,* and *always* appear on multiple-choice tests. Unless you *know* that a choice containing one of them is right, you can be fairly safe in guessing that it's wrong. If you can eliminate one or two answers as definitely wrong, you have fewer statements to keep in mind while trying to select the best one.

Be sure to remember *not* to practice any speed-reading techniques on quizzes! I have heard students reading review questions misread words in a way that completely changed the meaning of the questions. So read quizzes with extra care.

While you are taking a multiple-choice test, you may find that some questions require much more thought than others, and you may puzzle over two or three possible answers. Rather than spend too much time with such questions, put a mark in front of the question and go on. Then after you get through the rest of the test, go back and decide on the difficult questions you've skipped.

Even if the number of questions you miss is subtracted from the number you get right, the odds are in your favor if you answer every question—at least if you can narrow your choice of answers down to two or three. To prove this to students, I've had them go through old quizzes keeping two sets of answers. In one set they would leave blank the space for answers to questions they felt unsure of; in the other set, they would answer all the questions. They invariably made higher scores on the sets where they guessed at some of the answers.

If you have time to review your answers, by all means do so. But *be careful* about changing answers. I have had students tell me that they kept a list of the questions whose answers they changed on a test. Sometimes they changed as many as a half dozen from right to wrong, with only one or two from wrong to right.

If you find that you've misread part of a question the first time through the quiz and you're almost certain your first answer was wrong, change it. But if you are as uncertain on second reading as you were on the first, *don't* change your answer. For some reason, first guesses are more likely to be right than second ones. From reports of my students and from my own experience, I'd estimate that three out of four such changes are from right to wrong. So don't make any change in your multiple-choice answer unless you feel very certain you can justify it.

Just as it's helpful to know about trends in objective tests, it's also helpful to know what most teachers seem to look for in essays.

The day my European history teacher returned the first batch of quizzes, he told us (as I have written in my notes), "The best way to answer an essay-type question is to summarize the answer in one sentence and then give supporting information and argument. You need both generalizations and supporting details and particulars."

With this guideline, I examined my essays in the test to see where I met and where I fell short of the goal. You might benefit from analyzing one of the essays with me. A rather typical essay problem for a survey course in European history is: "Explain the chief means by which the kings began to overpower the nobles during the fifteenth and sixteenth centuries (15 mins.)."

Notice first that I copied the problem. It's good practice to write out an essay question. Perhaps it's better still to word the beginning of your essay so that it's clear what the question was. In that way you're more likely to get a sentence summary of your answer.

For my essay I spent a minute or two recalling points from notes and from what I'd read in the text and outside readings. Then I jotted down "marriage alliances, wars between countries, gunpowder, the court, revival of Roman law." I didn't include the points in an introductory sentence or paragraph, as my teacher would have preferred (I found out after the quiz). Instead I jumped into a paragraph on marriage alliances:

> The early means of the union of territories were marriage and political alliance of small territories. *[When I analyzed this after I got the test back, I decided the*

sentence was a satisfactory generalization.] This union gave more power to certain rulers, but usually until the fifteenth century they did not have much power beside that which the vassals were willing to give *[use of effect okay, I felt, but I should have used a specific example such as the combining of Aragon and Castile with the marriage of Ferdinand and Isabel]*.

However, in Spain first and later in France and England, inter-kingdom wars made it possible for kings to demand and get more power over the lesser lords *[pretty good transition from previous paragraph]*. Fighting the Moors in Spain, for example, caused a greater unity of purpose and a rise of national unity *[a good example to support the generalization]*. The nobles in such wars were willing to sacrifice something of their power for the greater good of the rising national kingdom *[effect]*.

The advent of gunpowder and its application made the old castles vulnerable *[generalization]*. The castle no longer gave the protection of the Middle Ages *[effect]*. With the use of gunpowder, kings who could obtain money could subdue *[cause]* the largest stronghold of lords *[effect of lack of protection of castles]*. This need for capital to buy guns and artillery *[cause]* led to a union of interests between the king and the rising middle class *[effect, political and economic change]*.

Another more subtle method of overpowering the nobles was to get them to come and live at the luxurious court of the kings *[good generalization]*. Thus separated from their land, the nobles were no longer much of a threat *[effect; this paragraph is weak because there is no specific example, such as the fact that Cardinal Richelieu started the practice in France, and Louis XIV brought it to near perfection]*.

Too, the kings began to dissolve ties between nobles and vassals and to make themselves sovereign *[fairly good generalization].* Political historians such as Nicolo Machiavelli *[detail]* were much read for their advocation of absolute sovereignty of the king *[supporting fact].* Historians such as Budé also revived old Roman law which gave more power to state and ruler. *[Details and supporting statements make this a better paragraph than the previous one.]*

By the total of such means, kings in Spain, France, and England became truly sovereign by the latter part of the fifteenth century *[fair summarizing conclusion].*

This essay answer is well enough organized and includes enough of the main points the teacher expected to earn me an *A-*. The lack of a one-sentence or paragraph summary of the answer at the beginning is partly offset by the inclusion of such a summary at the end. The lack of supporting details in the first and third paragraphs kept the essay from getting a full *A*. On later quizzes, I was more conscious of the need for supporting detail and statements—thanks to my professor's emphasizing the point.

Good generalizations, combined with supporting detail and statements, are what all teachers seem to look for on essay examinations. So remember for your essays:

1) Select quickly the points you are going to develop *and have time to develop.*
2) Try to write a one-sentence or opening-paragraph summary of your answer.
3) Write a good generalization about each point in its own paragraph.
4) Give supporting details—dates, names, causes and effects, quotations (especially for literature courses)—for each generalization.
5) If you have time, write a conclusion that ties the points together again.

You may notice that the pattern is the same as the form of the "standard theme" discussed in an earlier chapter of this book.

Tests – from Two Points of View

While you are taking the test, you must glance at the clock occasionally and divide your time effectively among the different parts of your answers. I remember how this lesson was driven home to me.

On one of two fifteen-minute essays, I was to write about Simón Bolívar. I had read a biography of him as part of my outside reading, and I had trouble narrowing down my main points. As a result, I ended up spending twenty minutes on that essay. My teacher gave me an *A* on it, but I had only ten minutes for my second fifteen-minute essay, and I ended up with a *B* on it. I would have made a better grade if I hadn't known so much about Bolívar—or at least if I'd limited my essay on him. I did learn a lesson I've never forgotten.

If you want to make the best test score you're capable of, you have to study for the kind of quiz your teacher gives. Once I convinced myself I should study for an essay quiz on a survey course in Latin American literature, and my teacher surprised me with thirty short-answer and completion questions that demanded more minor details than I remembered. I made a *B* on the test. For the next one I thought of two or three possible essays, but I concentrated on preparing for another quiz like the first. This time I was not surprised. With no more work than I'd put out for the first test, I made an *A* on the second one.

You see the point, but don't carry it too far. Some teachers deliberately vary their tests, with or without warning, giving an objective test one time, an essay exam next—or a combination of both types. In such cases, you have to be prepared for any type of quiz.

Learning a little about objective and essay tests is the best medicine I know for relieving quiz nerves. The next best remedy is to realize that tests may be a good experience for you and that a little nervous tension kept under control can be more of a help than a hindrance at quiz time.

I know about the kind of tension that is a hindrance to good test performance. I've felt butterflies in my stomach. I've noted a tightening in my neck and shoulders and a tremor in a sweaty hand. But most of my excess tension was in grammar school and early high school. By the time I reached college, I knew myself well enough to realize something I would repeat to myself before a difficult quiz: "If I had three more weeks to prepare for this test, I probably wouldn't be any better prepared. What I'll do will be pretty close to the best I'm capable of now. So try to do your best, Blaylock, and no excuses!"

Sometimes I wonder if some students don't build up tension in themselves as an excuse for bad results if they should come. Maybe they are afraid to accept the results of tests as the best they can do. To protect their egos, they'd rather prepare inadequately, build up tension worrying about a test, and make a *C*, perhaps, than be satisfied with a *B*, admitting the fact that they are not yet capable of making an *A*.

Honesty with oneself, then, is a key step toward relaxing the tension brought on by the fear of tests. No one really knows his own or another person's potential. But it is a great relief to finish a quiz—even one where you weren't quite perfect—with the feeling, "Well, I've done just about the best I'm now capable of doing."

For heaven's sake, don't get the idea that teachers enjoy marking mistakes. There may be a few fiendish exceptions, but most teachers are either too busy or too lazy to prefer grading a bad paper where they must do a lot of close reading and writing. Even on objective tests, it takes longer to grade a test with many mistakes than one with only a few. And a bad essay test may take two or three times as long to grade as a good one.

By the time a teacher gets through reading a batch of essay tests, assigning grades often becomes a matter of reward and punishment. The students with the poorest essays are punished with *D's* and *F's* because they have caused the teacher so much work. The authors of the best papers are rewarded with *A's* and *B's* because their essays have taken the least effort to mark and comment upon.

For teachers, too, tests are a lot of work. In many courses where the classes are small enough for class discussion and the teachers have a chance to observe the students, they know pretty well how students are going to perform on the quizzes. There are exceptions, of course. Just as some athletes can perform their best only under game conditions, a few students do their best only under the stress of examinations.

Tests, then, are not even primarily for the benefit of teachers in deciding on the grade to give their students. Believe it or not, tests benefit primarily the students. Tests give you practice in coping with tension. They cause you to think more about the course material, to work harder at organizing it into patterns that are meaningful to you. They give you practice in making generalizations from facts and in supporting generalizations with facts you recall.

As Dr. Moorhead, a history teacher of mine, once explained it: "If you can make intelligent generalizations at the time of a quiz and can support them with facts, you'll probably be able to remember the generalizations years after you have forgotten the supporting facts. But if you can't support generalizations with facts at quiz time, soon you'll forget the generalizations and remember almost nothing from the course."

Essay tests, particularly, give you important practice in organizing and projecting what you've learned. Whether you can make use of facts and ideas is the final test of knowledge.

Whether you like it or not, ours is a competitive society. Competition on the football gridiron, the baseball diamond, and the race track gets the major attention of our society. But most of the competition is really in making spoken and written decisions under pressure. Often, though not always, the people who star under the pressure of classroom examinations go on to star in business or the professions.

You shouldn't have to wait until you get a quiz back in order to decide how you did on it. You should rate your own performance with questions like these: Did I prepare myself for the test about as well as I knew how in the time I had? Did I let myself think about and organize what I was learning in terms of my own experience and background? Did I make use of both my facts and my intuition in answering multiple-choice tests? Did I organize and project my essay answers the best way I could? Did I get so involved with the challenge of the test that I forgot to be nervous?

If you can answer "yes" to these questions, you'll not only feel good about a test, but chances are your teacher will give you a good grade, too.

Most students I've known who made *A's* regularly seemed less concerned about grades than other students did. Yes, they studied hard, they knew the tricks of taking tests and of writing teacher-pleasing essays, but they didn't worry much about grades. They believed that if they studied to learn the material and prepared themselves for the tests, they could handle the tests when they came.

One of the best ways to conquer and control tension over quizzes is to study as well as you can reasonably expect of yourself and then push the thought of grades as far from your mind as you can. The tension involved in a determination to make a *B* on a test, for example, may be just the factor that keeps a student from making the grade he's hoping for. The reason for this is that as soon as a student starts bucking for a grade, he tends to reduce a subject to its dead objective aspect. A final grade is a sort of epitaph to a course. (If a student is more interested in grades than what he learns, maybe he ought to get a job as clerk in the office of admissions and records.)

You can push the thought of grades out of your mind—at least while you study—by concentrating on the vitality of a subject, by breathing some spirit into it so that it will come alive for you. Finding ways to do this is the main purpose of this book.

Another way to avoid excess tension on a particular test is to

190

realize that the score you make probably won't make much difference five or ten years from now, anyway. It's true that the score you make on some tests may even cause you to change your major—either away from or toward the subject of the test. But you probably won't know which test is the critical one *before* you take it. One thing is certain: Too much or too little tension keeps you from doing your best.

Chances are good, though, that you don't have to worry about relaxing too much—without tranquilizers. I'd wager that for every student who is a little too relaxed to do his best on a test, there are seven who are too tense, and maybe two who are feeling about the right amount of tension.

Tension under control is good. I have written essays in fifty minutes under the pressure of a test that I couldn't surpass in two hours in the relaxation of my room or the library.

Remember that a little tension at quiz time is good if you can make it *serve* you. To do so, I suggest the following:

1) Prepare the best you can, benefitting from the study suggestions in this book.
2) Glance over your notes and text the night and/or the morning before your quiz.
3) Admit that you probably wouldn't do much better if you had more time to prepare.
4) Realize that the test probably isn't as important as you fear.
5) Resolve to do your best and not to be ashamed of the results.
6) Before you start the test, take a half dozen deep breaths, say a silent prayer perhaps, and notice that most of the students are more nervous than you are.
7) Remember that the teachers dislike exams almost as much as you do.

Finally, remember that when you finish the test, your professor's work on the exam has scarcely begun—even if, as is highly unlikely, he waits until midnight and grades the tests by tossing the exam books up the basement steps.

CHAPTER 16

ALL IN GOOD TIME

A lot of students could scarcely believe it when my college's "morning astonisher" included Ted in its list of junior Phi Beta Kappas. Few had known that Ted had made all *A's* during his first five semesters. Now he was the talk of the campus and the student union.

"Why, I didn't think he ever studied," said one of the girls he dated occasionally, shaking her head. "I've never seen him at the library at night since we started here together as freshmen."

"I thought he was pretty bright," her male companion commented, picking up his cup of hot coffee. "He's never missed a meeting of the physics club, and I understand he's been elected president of his fraternity for next year."

"And that usually means a person has been a pretty active member," the co-ed interrupted. "All those activities, and grades like that? I can still hardly believe it." She shook her head again.

"Well, it couldn't happen to a nicer guy," her date said with a grin. "I guess he must find time to study sometime." He glanced toward the table where I was having a cup of coffee, and I nodded to him.

I could have enlightened them a little. But I didn't want to disillusion the girl. I knew Ted did study.

I saw him three days a week in the physics library, where I went between a physics and a philosophy class. And I never saw a boy working more studiously than Ted.

He was either alone at a desk working a problem or searching in the stacks for a book or a science journal. He always seemed completely absorbed in what he was doing.

The girl and boy at the union knew Ted socially and in extracurricular activities. I was acquainted with him as a fellow student in the physics library. Like the best-adjusted students, Ted could both play hard and study hard.

A couple of weeks after he was elected to Phi Beta Kappa with his straight *A's*, Ted disclosed part of his secret to an inquiring reporter from our college's daily. Quite rightly, the reporter guessed that Ted would be able to pass along some helpful ideas to other students, particularly freshmen.

Ted told the reporter that his key to good academic work was the way he organized his time. He said he didn't like to waste his time deciding every few minutes or hours what he was going to do; so he planned his study time so that he could do nearly all of it between eight o'clock in the morning and five or six in the afternoon.

His studies finished before dinner, Ted enjoyed his evenings without feeling that he ought to be in his room or at the library studying. In other words, he studied when he studied, and he played when he played.

All this doesn't mean that you ought to do all of *your* studying during the day. It may be that you study best at night and that the best time for your recreation is in the afternoon. But Ted's main point is still valid: You need to get your time organized so you don't have to make too many little decisions.

However well you may organize your time, you might not

make straight *A 's,* as Ted did. But I guarantee you one thing: If you get your time organized so that you can spend a reasonable number of hours both in study and in recreation, you'll enjoy and benefit from school much more.

Making the best use of your time requires three steps. First, plan what studying you intend to do for a whole week. Second, keep a record of the number of hours you have actually studied in each course. And, third, analyze your performance and your new assignments, and then make plans for the following week.

For the planning step, you might take a large sheet of paper, say 8½-by-11 inches. Divide the long side into seven columns of 1½ inch width, and label them with the days of the week. Now rule off the paper into three-eighths-inch widths parallel to the long side. On the left-hand margin, label hours from six A.M. to one A.M. Now mark in all your time already scheduled for classes, laboratories, meal times, committee meetings, and so forth. Somewhere in the time remaining you have to plan your study, your recreation, and perhaps part of your sleep.

"What is a reasonable number of hours to study in college?" you might ask. The rule of thumb at my university is two hours of study or laboratory per week for each semester hour's credit. For example, if you are enrolled in fifteen lecture hours a week with no laboratory course, such as chemistry or physics, your quota of study is thirty hours a week outside of class. If you average eight hours of classes and study each day, you need to work only five hours on weekends to meet the suggested quota.

But for some courses you may have to study more than two hours for each hour in class, and in other courses you may be able to do good work with less study than that. When I was a college sophomore, I was enrolled in a five-hour physics course and a five-hour beginning Latin course, plus a couple of other courses. Since I'd already studied French and Spanish and knew how to study languages pretty effectively, I had to spend only about an hour a day on Latin. But I hadn't studied much science, and I had only the minimum amount of math required for physics; so I averaged closer to three hours of study in physics for each hour of lecture.

If you know, for instance, that math is harder for you than a foreign language, you might plan at first two and a half hours of study for each math class and an hour and a half for the foreign language. If you can't even guess how much study a course will take for you, use the estimate of two hours of reading and study for each lecture period. Then you can modify your plans as you find out more about how much you can accomplish in your study time and as you find out more about each course.

Try to plan to study your courses in a set order each day, and keep your favorite course for the last. Suppose you have a three-hour study hall or you plan to study for three hours in the library on Monday, Wednesday, and Thursday afternoons. Perhaps you plan to study French, math, and history those afternoons.

Suppose you like to study French most, history somewhat less, and math least of all. I would suggest that you begin your afternoon of study with history, the course you like tolerably well. Then after about fifty minutes, take a ten-minute break and then begin work on your math. After another fifty minutes, switch to your favorite of the three courses, as a sort of dessert.

Of course, you don't want to watch the clock so closely that you stop reading history two or three pages from the end of the chapter or stop working on your math a couple of problems from the end of the assignment. It might even be that you work only on your history and math—even though you planned to work on all three courses—and that you keep the French for the evening. In short, you shouldn't try to follow a study plan slavishly.

The idea of studying your subjects in a certain order and keeping your favorite subject for the last is a good one, however. The reason for this becomes clear when you think about it. Before realizing what is happening, many students get into the habit of putting off their most difficult subject to the last on their day's schedule. Tired when they reach it, they find that the subject seems even harder. After only a few minutes—before they really start concentrating on the subject—they begin to yawn or frown, and soon they give up and go to bed.

After a short while, they get back a bad quiz or two, and it becomes even harder to study the subject. Too quickly they are in danger of failing or barely passing the course.

If they adopt better study habits at this point, they have to study not only to learn the past and present assignments but also to overcome their acquired fear and dislike of the course.

So don't put off your most difficult course to the last. If you have a favorite subject that you save for the last in your study, it's much easier to do justice to all your courses. You may not be able to study any course very well when you're tired, but you can study a course you like twice as well as you can one you don't like.

Many students I've known have improved their college work simply by planning to have breakfast before their first class—and sticking to this plan. You may be able to stagger into a class fifteen minutes after your alarm clock goes off, but you're not likely to get much out of the lecture. By eating breakfast before your first class, you can be much wider awake and more alert for that class.

I'm convinced that the breakfast habit is one reason that students who grow up on farms tend to do better in college than what might be expected of them. Research studies have shown that children and teen-agers who eat breakfast perform better in school.

I feel sure that the same results hold true for college students, perhaps to an even stronger degree. The student who gets up for breakfast demonstrates a bit of self-discipline. If he can find time in his busy day for breakfast, chances are that he can find time for his studies, for recreation, and for the extracurricular activities that are an important part of his education. By getting up for breakfast, you can start your classwork refreshed and alert. And you will have energy to last you until your next meal. A large percentage of college students don't eat breakfast regularly, but you'll be much better off if you do.

You'll also be better off if you plan to get sufficient sleep. You probably have a good idea of whether you need six, seven, eight, or nine hours of sleep to feel well and to work effectively. You'd better plan regularly to get within an hour of the amount of sleep you seem to require.

Getting enough sleep seems to be a problem in every college. The best way I know of doing it is by planning your studies so that you can take care of most of your work during the day. Then, if you are in a dormitory, you can get to sleep while many students are still trying to make themselves study. You may find that a thirty-minute nap at noon or early in the afternoon can do wonders to refresh you.

In addition to sufficient sleep, you need time for recreation. Plan some time for sports or relaxation in the afternoons or evenings. It's true that too much work can make a person stale. Sometimes the students who plan to study nine or ten hours a day end up studying two or three—not that they shouldn't study more. The students who set a reasonable goal are much more likely to develop effective study habits.

One way to make sure that you study as many hours as you plan to is by scheduling make-up time for any failure to meet your quota of hours. In most colleges, Friday afternoon seems to be a time for relaxing and "thanking God it's Friday." We call it TGIF day here. So you might reward yourself for studying well during the early part of the week by taking Friday afternoon off from school work—except classes and laboratory work, of course. But study on Friday afternoon as punishment for not keeping to your study plans earlier in the week. The point is that you should use a system of rewards and punishments on yourself.

You may find that by taking a five- or ten-minute break each hour of study you actually get more studying done. Some psychologists say that most people cannot effectively spend more than fifty minutes at a time in study. So why not plan to reward yourself with a ten-minute break about every hour of study? Get up, stretch, go for a drink of water—but resist the temptation to let the break last more than ten minutes. It takes will power at first, but soon such procedures become habit. Automatically you ready yourself to start concentrating again.

The planning step we've been discussing is just one of the three steps in making good use of your time. "The best laid schemes o'mice and men gang aft a-gley," as Robert Burns put it. Some of your plans are likely to go astray, too. You can seldom be sure that friends from home won't suddenly drop by to see you. Or you may become sick. Or some organization may make unexpected demands on your time. More important than what you plan to do is what you get done! So keep a record of how many hours you spend studying each course. This is the simplest of the three steps in making the best use of your time. It takes only a minute or so each night.

You might make a nightly ritual of marking the number of hours, to the nearest half hour, that you've spent in each of your courses. You could record them on a chart that you keep either above your study desk or in a notebook. It might look something like this:

Study in October

Week of	English	Algebra	Government	Chemistry
Oct. 2	ⅢⅠ II	ⅢⅠ I	ⅢⅠ	ⅢⅠ ⅢⅠ I
Oct. 9	ⅢⅠ I	ⅢⅠ II	ⅢⅠ I	ⅢⅠ ⅢⅠ
Oct. 16	ⅢⅠ I	ⅢⅠ III	ⅢⅠ I	ⅢⅠ ⅢⅠ I
Oct. 23	ⅢⅠ I	ⅢⅠ I	ⅢⅠ II	ⅢⅠ ⅢⅠ
Oct. 30				

By keeping a record of the number of hours you spend studying each course, you can immediately see which courses you're slighting. Students have a tendency to believe they are putting in more time on their harder courses than they actually are.

Possibly the most effective way of forcing yourself to learn to manage your time is by taking a correspondence course and having to do the assignments on schedule. I did two and a half years of high-school work by correspondence study. And, believe me, I would never have gotten it done in two and a half years if I hadn't planned my study and kept a record of the number of hours I spent working on each course. In order to stay on schedule, I found it necessary to have both a flexible plan of study and a record of time spent.

By looking at the record, I decided how much time I probably needed to study the next week in order to stay on schedule. Making this decision was for me the third step in organizing my time, the analysis step.

How many hours you spend studying a course is more important than how many hours you planned to study. Similarly, how much you actually accomplish is more important than the number of hours you study. So near the end of each weekend, on Sunday night perhaps, spend ten or fifteen minutes analyzing your study plan, your record of the number of hours you've studied each course, the way you've been able to keep up with assignments, and your new assignments. Then, in light of your analysis, revise your old plan of study for the next week. For example, if you find you've taken more time on your math than you originally planned, allow a little more time for that subject the next week.

And don't merely think about your analysis, write it down in a notebook, preferably the one that contains the record of the number of hours you study each course. In your half page or so of analysis of your study accomplishments and needs, include comments on any new study techniques you've tried.

You may find, for example, that the most effective time for you to study is not between eight o'clock in the morning and midnight, but between five and seven o'clock in the morning. Some students perform near their peak efficiency very early in the morning. Others don't hit their stride until the afternoon or perhaps late at night. You have to analyze yourself and your study experience to know in which category you belong.

What this sort of analysis amounts to is a kind of study diary, except that you write it up only once a week. Just as with a diary or your class notes, your analysis should be dated. The advantage of writing the analysis is similar to that of writing an essay examination. In projecting your thoughts onto paper, you tend to clarify and organize them. And you get them down in permanent form. As weeks pass, you can refer to earlier analyses and improve your ability to size up your study problems and your study habits.

The practice in analysis and writing is not only important to you now but may be even more important to you in the future. The three-step process of planning, recording, and analyzing your study performance is the best way I know to develop good study habits. What are good study habits? *Good study habits are those that work for you.* The only way you can decide intelligently whether or not a certain habit or technique of study is good for you is to try it and analyze your results.

Don't get the idea that this whole process of planning, recording, and analyzing your use of time is going to take very much time. It won't. Most of the time it does take will be during the first two or three weeks of a semester, the best time to establish good study habits.

In two or three weeks of studying and planning as we've been discussing in this book, you can develop good study habits that will enable you to keep up well in every subject throughout the semester. And one of these good habits will be the habit of planning, recording, and analyzing your use of time.

I feel confident that you'll consider the few minutes you

spend organizing and studying your use of time to be the most important minutes in your education. If students put out as much energy and concern during the first two weeks of a semester as they do during the last two, there would be far fewer drop-outs and flunk-outs from college. And far less midnight oil would be burned during exam week, when about the only thing the extra work does is to salve the conscience of students who've been negligent the first part of the semester.

Many students who fail to develop a good plan of study often fall victim to what doctors might call "the test syndrome." Victims of the test syndrome are jolly Janes and Jims until their first test is announced. Then they drop what little studying they've been doing except in the course they're to be tested in.

They study furiously, trying to catch up on the text and outside readings, if any. Madly they try to cram down their throats what the text says and what they find in their friends' notes or in old quizzes—all just to be able to regurgitate a few facts for the quiz.

In the meantime, assignments for other courses are neglected or forgotten. After the quiz, they may return to their jolly selves. No more worries until their next test is announced. Soon they are studying only for quizzes, which seem to come with a maddening frequency.

It's little wonder that victims of the test syndrome find their college education such a bitter and frustrating experience. The cure for the test syndrome is planned, regular study for each course. Then there is no need to try to cram three or four weeks of text and outside reading into a couple of nights.

Compare the victims of the test syndrome with college athletes who have to make their study time count. In spite of two or three hours of practice daily, and in spite of road trips and home games on weekends, football players often do extremely well in school in relation to their abilities and background. Sometimes people like to joke about dumb football players, but one of the best students I ever tutored was one of those "dumb" football players. In three years of pre-medical studies at the university, he made only three hours of *B* and the rest *A*. Yet his aptitude scores were not extraordinarily high. He just knew how to study and how to manage his time. He didn't have time to waste worrying about his studies and trying to decide what he had to do. When it came time for him to study each evening, he knew what he had to do and approximately how long it would take him, and he went directly to work.

It's the irritating little decisions, the back-breaking straws, that can make life miserable. A story of a farmer's hired hand shows this clearly. For weeks, the hired hand has been doing beautifully every job given to him. No one could plow a straighter furrow or build a better fence. One day, though, the farmer gave him the task of sorting potatoes. About an hour later he came dejectedly up to the farmer. "I quit," he said, shaking his head. "I just can't stand it. All them decisions is killing me."

I tell some of my students that they are too fond of making little decisions and exercising their will power. For example, a student who never cuts a class almost never thinks about whether he's going to class or not. It's almost automatic for him to go.

What all this discussion is boiling down to is this: Take care to form good habits, and good habits will take care of you.

Good study habits can be formed by a little planning, record-keeping, experimentation, and thought at the *beginning* of the semester. They take a little time to form and a little will power, but nothing I know of can contribute more to your happiness and to your performance in college. By planning your work and following your plan, you can find time to practice the suggestions on study in the earlier part of this book.

In summary, then,

All in Good Time

I. Plan
1) Make out a time table for your scheduled classes, study, recreation, and other activities for a week.
2) Allow enough hours of reading and study for each course.
3) Plan to get a reasonable amount of sleep.
4) Plan to get up in time for breakfast.
5) Plan to take a five- or ten-minute break during each hour of study.
6) Punish yourself for failure to live up to your plans by making yourself study extra hours on Friday or over the weekend.
7) Reward yourself for keeping up with your plans and your assignments by taking an occasional entire weekend off from study.

II. Record

Each evening, record in a notebook the number of hours (to the nearest half hour) you've spent working on each course.

III. Analyze

Consider your plan of study for the previous week, your record of performance, and your new assignments. Think of any new techniques of study you may have tried. Write a brief analysis in a small notebook, and revise your study plans for the next week accordingly.

I say again that one of the main advantages to this sort of planning is the amount of time it saves from making little decisions about when and what to study. I've known students who spent at least as much time fretting and worrying and talking about what they had to do as they spent actually studying. By avoiding this waste of time and energy, and by avoiding the "test syndrome," you make college much more pleasant, and you increase your chances of experiencing the joy, enlightenment, and satisfaction you can discover in dedicated and interested study. (There are no basically uninteresting subjects—only uninterested students.)

There's a saying, "If you want a job done, ask a busy man." You can find time in your day for all that you must do. It's a matter of organizing your time, of working when you work and playing when you play. It's a matter of doing all in good time.

Who knows, perhaps other students will be talking about what an effective student you are, too. Maybe it's not in you to be another Ted Webber, but effective organization and use of your time will take you much closer to your goal of becoming a good, well-rounded student, the goal that prompted you to read this book.

CHAPTER 17

Un-CLASSIFIED

You have covered a lot of ground in this book, and I hope you have felt a strong sense of direction.

You have let me point the way through the subject areas that most trouble college students—theme writing, foreign languages, basic math, and problem solving in the sciences. You have let me point the way around or over the obstacles all students face—exams, note-taking, reading and study, and organization of time to best advantage.

Perhaps you've not been content just to listen to the directions. Perhaps you've already put aside this book now and then to go and test for yourself its directions on theme writing or language study or problem solving. On the other hand, you may have read this book straight through, letting me point out the main features of college education before you go and see if I am guiding you aright.

In either case, I am about to take leave of you, but with the map and directions still in your hands. First though, I want to point out to you a few more features in the academic landscape, features that don't quite fit into the classifications of the earlier chapters. I want to make a few observations—some on my background—that may give you courage to face the road ahead, and perhaps even an eagerness to explore some of the nooks and crannies of that vast and awesome experience called college education.

First, let's consider further a major feature in that experience: the college teacher. How can you make the best use of your teachers, who must pass judgment on your qualities as a student in the courses they teach?

We've already covered the subjects of class notes, exams, and regular class attendance. The better you do at all these, the better it is for you. However, one matter that we've scarcely mentioned yet is the matter of getting acquainted with your teacher.

I think most teachers are flattered by the visit of a student who seems genuinely interested in the teacher's subject. So try to arrange for a conference with your teacher early in the semester, preferably before your first quiz. But, for heaven's sake, don't start your visit with the question, "How can I make a good grade in this course?" Instead, ask for suggestions about how to study effectively. (He might even give you a good idea or two we haven't covered in this book!) Let him talk to you about the value of his subject to your education. This should please him.

Don't avoid visiting your teacher because you're afraid he'll think you're apple polishing. He may. But he will appreciate it if you can stay away from the subject of grades.

"Why go to see a teacher at all if you don't show concern for your grade?" you may ask. You should go for two main reasons. Most teachers are interested in seeing that you do good work, and you will probably realize this much more clearly after a visit with your teacher in his office. Feeling that a teacher wants you to do well, you are likely to study harder and feel more eager to learn. Also, the more students a teacher knows, the better the learning atmosphere in the classroom is likely to be.

One semester in my undergraduate days, an English teacher of mine made appointments to see all of his students the first two weeks of the summer session. The visits were quite casual. He asked where we were from, what our majors were, what we planned to do after graduation. The interest he showed in us as individuals sparked the class and helped make it one of the best classes I've ever been in. I had two other classes with the same gravel-voiced teacher, but in neither did he schedule conferences with all his students. I'm convinced that far more teachers should make the effort to get acquainted with their students, as this English professor did the first summer I had him. You don't have to wait for the teacher to suggest a conference; you can ask to have a conference with him.

But you may be thinking of the French professor I mentioned in the first chapter on language study, whom one of my students asked for suggestions on how to study French. His reply was, you may remember, "Have you ever tried opening the book?" I think the chance of getting that sort of reply is very slim, and I believe you stand to benefit considerably by having a conference with your teacher. The good that may come of it is well worth the risk of embarrassment.

Of course, you have to show a little consideration. If in your conference your teacher keeps toying with his hat or otherwise seems in a hurry to leave for his coffee break, you should try to beat a fairly hasty retreat. Let's face it, some teachers just don't care to see students, because they are not very concerned with teaching. Most, however, are glad to get acquainted with students who show interest in their course.

Suppose, though, that you do have a teacher you consider arrogant, domineering, unfair, disinterested in his students—and you can't get out of his class. What's the best attitude you can have toward such a person? It's probably best for you to consider the teacher as just another of the difficult problems in human relationships you'll face throughout your life. Look at it as a type of problem you need practice in coping with—and start practicing!

Try to understand the man. Does he think he should be teaching at Harvard or Yale instead of at your school? Maybe he suffers from the common feeling that no one appreciates him as much as he deserves.

Maybe, though, you just can't get acquainted with him. Perhaps he thinks all students are apple polishers and shoos out of his office any student who tries to have a conference with him. What can you do then?

If your teacher is among the worst, you can at least determine to learn as much as you can *in spite* of him or *to spite* him. Show him that you are a better student than he deserves.

The easy solution to the problem of the difficult teacher is to quit studying, to accept a poor or failing grade, and then to blame your teacher for it. But whom do you hurt with this sort of solution? The teacher may even be happy to give you a poor grade, but I doubt if you'd be very happy to accept it.

The best solution to the problem of the disagreeable teacher is a determination to learn the subject with or without much help from him. Consider him the enemy team. Take careful notes. Try to find out what he wants on quizzes. Do your best, and it just may be that you'll decide the teacher you disliked is not as bad as you thought. Even if he is that bad, you still have profited: You've won the game.

It's surprising how often we graduates have changed our opinions of our teachers over the years. Looking back, we often feel that some of our best teachers were those we thought most difficult and unbearable at the time we had them. Often we look back with contempt on the teachers who won our affection at the time by giving us plenty of class cuts and easy grades.

So it may be that the teacher you now detest most is the very one who will have the most lasting and most favorable influence on your life.

The same thing is true of subjects. Who can really be sure which courses he'll use later in making his living? Many history majors, for example, end up as insurance salesmen. Many engineering students become business executives.

I pity the student who keeps worrying about whether or not the ideas he learns in a course will help him make money. Such worry only makes the course harder to learn, because it takes the fun out of learning. Besides, college administrators aren't likely to change course requirements just because a few students can't see any connection between the business world, for example, and the study of Chaucer and Shakespeare.

You are not going to change your college's course requirements for a particular major. So when you are enrolled in a course, you might as well make up your mind to learn as much as you can, hoping that what you learn will either help you make a living or make living more worthwhile.

Sometimes psychologists speak of the carry-over value of courses. Too often they ignore the most important aspect of this carry-over, your attitude toward a course. If you take a course that seems very difficult to you at first and you master its principles, you finish the course with a greater respect for your ability to learn. As a result, other courses that are supposed to be difficult seem less frightening.

One of the most important characteristics a student can have is a good attitude toward education, toward learning, and toward life in general. Attitude, sense of direction, orientation, motivation—these are all related ideas. And often they tie in with religious experience and belief.

A number of times I have referred in this book to my taking courses by correspondence study and to using a wheelchair. Both came about as a result of a hunting accident during Christmas vacation the year I was fourteen and a sophomore in high school. The gun-shot wound damaged my spinal cord and left my legs paralyzed.

I feel sure that I would have died had I not had a religious conviction that life has purpose and meaning. That, along with a belief that someday I would walk again into Hammon High School, helped sustain me for three years. I read a great deal and studied Spanish, but I had no specific plans to try to use what abilities I still possessed.

Finally, after an unsuccessful spinal operation, my doctor told me that there was no hope that I would ever regain use of my legs. But he did hold out the possibility that I might go to college either on crutches or in a wheelchair.

I had to face the truth at last. This was the day I resolved to finish high school by correspondence study out on our farm and, God willing, to go to college.

Naturally I had wanted to get well and finish high school at Hammon. But I had to turn my back on this dream and start working with the abilities I had. Once the practical goal of finishing high school was fixed, it was relatively easy to set up my study schedules, keep records of the hours I studied, and learn to stick closely to my schedule. In two years, I did two years of high-school work.

After I finished high school, I had more operations that did not enable me to walk with crutches but did make it easier for me to attend college in a wheelchair.

I had done good high-school work. Now with the help of scholarships and the sacrifices of my parents, I was able to take clear aim at the once-hazy goal of graduating from college. The willingness of others to make sacrifices for me and to take chances on me tremendously increased my sense of responsibility. I felt I couldn't let them down. To me college education was never something I took for granted. It was a privilege and a responsibility.

I wasn't perfectly sure what I was going to do with a college education. I went to college with an open mind as far as a career was concerned. I supposed I would go into some occupation where I could use my ability for learning foreign languages. But when I took zoology, I let myself believe that I might follow a career in biology. When I studied physics the year I was a sophomore, I toyed with the idea of becoming a theoretical physicist. When I studied philosophy, I enjoyed the enlightenment it brought me, and I felt it provided background for any other academic subject I might study. Maybe I was fooling myself a bit, but I succeeded in enjoying every course I took, and that made studying a lot easier.

Questioning the value of a course you have to take only makes it harder. Anyway, the better you do in the course, the more effective your criticism will be–*after* the course is finished. If a student has made an *A* or *B* in a course and says it has little value, his criticism is more likely to be listened to than that of a student who fails or barely passes. Why waste energy cursing the powers-that-be for requiring you to take a certain course? You'll be much happier using the energy to study.

Admittedly, some courses are harder for a student than other courses. The nature of the difficulty differs. For example, you have to do more memorizing for chemistry than for physics, but elementary chemistry problems are easier to solve than physics problems. As zoology and botany are taught in my college, you have to memorize more for botany, and you have to learn to think a little more precisely and scientifically for zoology.

In any course, though, your desire to learn is a key factor. One of the better students I have tutored made half *C*'s and half *B*'s with tutorial help her first semester in college. Her second semester she made all *B*'s. This was the level of performance one might expect from Mary's scores on placement tests. But the third semester I tutored her, she made ten hours of *A* and only five of *B*. Now she was really developing good study habits and confidence in her ability to learn. Later, in her junior and senior years, she made two semesters of straight *A* without a tutor in the difficult major of laboratory technology.

My point is that neither you nor anyone else can be

completely sure of your abilities. Who can be certain that even Shakespeare or Newton or Einstein lived up to his full potential? You have abilities that you have scarcely begun to tap. What they are no one will know until you get busy, find them, and use them.

To approach the limits of your potential, you have to learn to organize and make good use of your time. You have to fan the spark of curiosity that smolders within you. You have to learn to divide your time wisely between studies and recreation, between time you allot to yourself and time you spend with friends. And remember that, while you'll know few of your college friends for more than four years, you have to live with yourself the rest of your life.

If you have yet to learn to discipline yourself, to face up to your responsibilities to yourself and to society, it may seem a little difficult at first to put into practice the principles and suggestions of this book. But, believe me, the personal satisfactions from doing so are more than ample rewards for your efforts. You will come closer to attaining personal freedom, which lies largely in an awareness and joyful acceptance of potentialities and responsibilities for good that are uniquely your own.

You will experience greater freedom of the spirit. A great religious teacher once said, "Ye shall know the truth, and the truth shall make you free." The more I have pondered the statement, the more I have come to believe that the *truth* in question is not so much the attainment of some goal as the process of seeking it. Perhaps truth lies in your seeking what is good in light of your responsibility to yourself and to mankind. We were taught a similar idea in the language of sports: "It matters not so much whether we win or lose, but how we play the game."

It has been my privilege to suggest how I believe the game of study, the game of learning, may be played most effectively and may bring the greatest satisfaction. I have tried to point out some of the best ways to go about studying and learning. But you must take the steps; the work is yours, and the rewards for your efforts are yours.

In all your efforts, try your best to develop and keep an eager sense of wonder. There is no end to learning, no end to the joy of discovering something interesting and exciting that you haven't known before. Even a child—or, perhaps, *especially* a child—can sense some of Sir Isaac Newton's enthusiasm when he said: "I do not know what I may seem to the world; but to myself I seem to have been only a boy playing on the seashore and diverting myself now and then finding a smoother pebble or a prettier shell than ordinary, whilst the great ocean of truth lay all undiscovered before me."

On one of the buildings at the Massachusetts Institute of Technology is a motto: "The larger the island of knowledge, the longer the shoreline of wonder." I hope this book is already helping you enlarge *your* island of knowledge and lengthen *your* shoreline of wonder. May you often experience the pleasure of finding for yourself smooth pebbles and pretty shells, even if someone has discovered them before you.